THINK GLOBALLY, ACT LOCALLY

Think Globally, Act Locally

The United Nations and the Peace Movements

Ken Coates

SPOKESMAN

First published in 1988 by:
Spokesman
Bertrand Russell House
Gamble Street
Nottingham, England
Tel. 0602 708318

Copyright © Spokesman

This book is copyright under the Berne Convention. All rights are reserved. Apart from any fair dealing for the purpose of private study, research, criticism or review, as permitted under the Copyright Act, 1956, no part of this publication may be reproduced, stored in a retrieval system, or transmitted, in any form or by any means, electronic, electrical, chemical, mechanical, photocopying, recording or otherwise, without the prior permission of the copyright owner. Enquiries should be addressed to the publishers.

British Library Cataloguing in Publication Data

Coates, Ken, *1930-*
   Think globally, act locally: the United Nations and the peace movements.
   1. Peace movements. Role of United Nations
   I. Title
   327.1'72

ISBN 0-85124-503-X
ISBN 0-85124-504-8 Pbk

Printed by the Russell Press Ltd, Nottingham
(Tel. 0602 784505)

Contents

Introduction		7
1	Combining Against Nuclear Proliferation	13
2	Can Nuclear-Free Zones be Enforceable?	62
3	Israel's Bomb: The First Victim	79
4	Peace, Rights and Freedom	100
5	European Nationalism and World Co-operation	112
6	NATO and the International Court	125
7	Reform of the United Nations	139
Appendix I: Support for Reform		152
Appendix II: The Attack on the United Nations		157

Introduction

"There are more hungry people in the world today, than ever before in human history, and their numbers are growing. In 1980, there were 340 million people in 87 developing countries not getting enough calories to prevent stunted growth and serious health risks ... the world bank predicts that these numbers are likely to go on growing".

Gro Harlem Brundtland, the Prime Minister of Norway, started out from facts like this in preparing her World Commission on the Environment, whose report, *Our Common Future*, was one of the most significant events of 1987. The experts of this Commission were aware that they were facing a global challenge. Human misery constitutes but one dimension of this challenge: or, it would be truer to say, constitutes but one dimension of this generation's experience of disorder. It is other generations, soon to arrive, who will experience the full consequences of our present misdeeds.

The worst victims of poverty are caught in a fearsome crisis of debt. But even those countries which are far above this threshold find they have mortgaged their future development in order to pay for their past expansion. Much of the debt of the South was incurred by military dictatorships. It is now imposed on new democracies. It is also worsened by high US interest rates which reflect the cost of the Strategic Defence Initiative and the biggest arms build-up in American peace-time history. This defence spending militates against development. If the debtors joined to exert combined bargaining power they could remedy this situation. For, as Keynes said, owing the bank £100 is your problem; owing it £1 million is the banker's problem. Now that developing countries owe well over $1 trillion it is a common problem for both the North and South which needs a joint international initiative to resolve it.

The world debt crisis accelerates the spoliation of natural resources. Irreplaceable rain forests are uprooted for quick profit, destroying whole species in the process. The elimination of species wastes inestimable resources laid up during the entire span of evolution. Millions of years of struggle and adjustment can be wiped away in order to secure a petty improvement in the value of exports. Who has time to weigh the balance of life when the creditor knocks? In Madagascar 93 per cent of the original forest has gone, and this means that probably 6,000 varieties of plants have been killed off. Each was once unique. Lake Malawi is being rapidly poisoned, imperilling the future of more than 500 species of fish. In Western Ecuador, almost all the primal forests have given way to plantations of bananas, or oil wells.

> "The number of species thus eliminated ... could well number 50,000 or more — all in just twenty-five years".

The wetlands of Brazil are similarly imperilled.

All this cutting and clearing, bulldozing and burning, contributes to profound atmospheric change culminating in what the scientists have styled "the greenhouse effect". As the planet heats up, so future food production becomes more problematic. Before some of our grandchildren are thinking about their pensions, the icecaps will be melting, and the waters will be rising around our coastal plains and cities.

Of course, before 1987, many young people were by no means convinced that there was any chance that such problems would come to fruition, since it was widely supposed that an inevitable war would have carried off most human beings long before they had any time to evaluate the effects of this mess. But the Washington summit, for the first time ever, agreed on measures of real disarmament, actually removing an entire category of nuclear weapons from deployment. Modest though this measure of disarmament must be adjudged to be, when weighed against the vast accumulations of strategic missiles, none the less it represented a most significant shift in the assumptions of military planning. Hope was once again in order, and might just possibly become fashionable.

Two years before the Brundtland Commission announced its findings, the Socialist International had published its own *Global Challenge*, its first major report on international economic policy, presented under the auspices of Michael Manley and Willy Brandt. This set out a simple agenda:

> "Our answer to militarism, monetarism and the transnational trend of trade and payments is clear. We need recovery and global spending, a restructuring of finance and trade, and a major redistribution of resources if we are to make possible a process of self-reinforcing, sustained social development into the twenty-first century."

None of this is easy. "At present", say the Socialist International's spokesmen, "it is blocked by some of the most powerfully vested interests in the world economy".

Why do we experience these warnings, one after another? Increasingly, they come from international teams of specialists, or political collaborators. It seems that, beneath the surface of these great difficulties in the management of the natural environment or the social economy there lies an even deeper crisis: the crisis of national democracy. Following the victory in the second world war, democratic advance had taken place over a very wide area of the world. Always imperfect, it was often ambiguous and sometimes badly flawed. But in the advanced countries, resting on two or three decades of relatively full employment, it provided a long expansion of broadly consensual constitutional development. During the same years, anti-colonial movements grew stronger and then triumphed, and their latest victories undermined the last centres of autocratic power in Europe.

The post-war economic arrangements which guaranteed stable expansion and a secure political consensus were also responsible for encouraging another development, however. They provided fertile soil for the growth of multinational capital, and thus launched business organization to a new level of power, unmatched by any purely national degree of sovereignty.

Multinational companies can run faster than the separate public health and conservation services of mere states. Macro-economic management is increasingly powerless at the national level, unless it follows directly on the trends determined in the interaction of global companies. Welfare infrastructures cannot find international linkages to enable them to escape the resultant national pressures for cuts and restrictions at every level. The grander big enterprise becomes, the shoddier the social fabric of education, health and welfare is likely to remain. In the poor countries debt and hunger rage. People are in open crisis. This is why, whichever way we turn, we now find that global problems present themselves, and reproach the inadequacies of our national democracies ever more keenly.

None of this process is confined to the capitalist democracies. A parallel development within the same world market has brought the Soviet Union and

Introduction

China to face the same global crisis. And that is why one of the most important attempts to explain the interconnections which are involved in this crisis was made by Mikhail Gorbachev, in his letter to the United Nations General Assembly of August 1987. This was subsequently published in *Pravda* on September 17th.

Here, Gorbachev was taking the theme of his democratic restructuring in the Soviet Union itself, *Perestroika*, and applying it to the international institutions which are the only inadequate existing mechanisms through which co-operation might be organized at anything like an appropriate scale. Over decades, the majority of nations have agreed on the need for a new international economic order. The Socialist Parties of Western Europe and Latin America are welcome supporters of this call, but they were by no means the first to launch it. Before them, the non-aligned states had agreed extensive proposals, designed to protect their interest in the outcome. The explosion of international debt has underlined the need for co-ordinated action, without providing any halfway to adequate machinery through which it could be organized.

Political will in the modern world is formed in accordance with national interests expressed through national organizations and shaped by states. How can we possibly arouse a proper response to world-wide issues if we cannot begin to transcend these limitations of our given political structures?

Evidently, Perestroika is one thing. The Global Challenge is another, which obtained the support of more than its core 84 Parties. *Our Common Future* sought to distill its findings from a whole directory of scientists and specialists scattered all around the planet, but it is only necessary to perceive the vastness of the tasks which it seeks to confront in order to realize the scope of the joint action that will be needed if this is to be done.

Linkage between all these separate initiatives seems indispensable to the success of any one of them. The closer the linkage, the greater reinforcement of success. Co-operation has already begun. A wide variety of Non-Governmental Organisations and Peace movements are exploring the networking of their efforts on all these issues. But the more these efforts succeed, the more evidently it becomes necessary to create appropriate changes in the official institutions of co-operation, and above all in the United Nations

These papers all begin with questions which have troubled the peace movements. All arrive at the need for institutional reforms, although each has found that need at the end of a different road.

1

Combining Against Nuclear Proliferation

The first United Nations Special Session on Disarmament, convened in New York in 1978, excited world opinion by reaching agreement on the goal of "general and complete disarmament". This goal was deliberately coupled with a series of intermediate objectives. One of these concerned the establishment of nuclear-weapon-free zones. Article 33 of the final statement of the 1978 Special Session commends the idea of such zones "on the basis of agreements or arrangements freely arrived at among the states of the zone concerned" and goes on to state that both the act of initiating such agreements and the act of recognising and respecting them, "constitute an important disarmament measure."

Later the declaration goes on to spell out this commitment in a little more detail. It begins with a repetition:

> "The establishment of nuclear-weapons-free zones on the basis of arrangements freely arrived at among the states of the region concerned, constitutes an important disarmament measure,"[1]

and then continues:

> "The process of establishing such zones in different parts of the world should be encouraged with the ultimate objective of achieving a world entirely free of nuclear weapons. In the process of establishing such zones, the characteristics of each region should be taken into account. The states participating in such zones should undertake to comply fully with all the objectives, purposes and principles of the agreements or arrangements establishing the zones, thus ensuring that they are genuinely free from nuclear weapons.

With respect to such zones, the nuclear-weapon states in turn are called upon to give undertakings, the modalities of which are to be negotiated with the competent authority of each zone, in particular:
a) to respect strictly the status of the nuclear-free zone;
b) to refrain from the use or threat of use of nuclear weapons against the states of the zone . . .

States of the region should solemnly declare that they will refrain on a reciprocal basis from producing, acquiring, or in any other way, possessing nuclear explosive devices, and from permitting the stationing of nuclear weapons on their territory by any third party and agree to place all their nuclear activities under International Atomic Energy Agency safeguards."

Of course, the final document of the Special Session is not beyond criticism. It is quite possible to identify a number of problems to which the document gives no attention, or inadequate attention. These become apparent even in the discussion about the establishment of nuclear-free zones. But that discussion itself owes a very great deal to the fact that agreement was reached in New York in 1978 and although no-one would suggest that there now exists a panacea for controlling and reversing the arms race, nonetheless the Special Session has offered us a groundwork for the development of nuclear-free zones.

There are two generally recognized forms of nuclear weapons proliferation: vertical proliferation of nuclear weapons in the arsenals of the two great powers, and horizontal proliferation of nuclear weaponry into the hands of new, formerly non-nuclear powers. Both are very dangerous, but few would deny that the greatest peril comes from vertical proliferation[2]. The Non-Proliferation Treaty, which came into force in 1970, commits 122 nations to refrain from manufacturing nuclear weapons. Three other states, the consenting nuclear powers, have endorsed the Treaty as states already in possession of nuclear weapons before the date of its conclusion. Other nuclear states exist, of course, but until recently none of them had endorsed the Treaty. The three of its signatories who are nuclear armed are thus committed, amongst other things to:

(a) negotiate an end to the nuclear arms race and a Treaty on Disarmament, and
(b) refrain from transferring nuclear weapons to other nations.

The signatory nuclear States could all therefore be considered to be in breach of the NPT, because the arms race roars ahead, nuclear weapons are deployed in forward positions on the territory of other States, and until 1987 the latest Treaty on arms control remained unratified in the United States. Not unnaturally, therefore, the NPT is in an unhealthy condition. Indeed, in 1980, the Treaty's review conference specifically underlined this fact. The last review conference in 1985 faced a situation in which matters had simply worsened, although the hopes for an impending summit meeting temporarily served to relax the confrontation between nuclear haves and have-nots.

By contrast with the Non-Proliferation Treaty, Nuclear-Free Zones possess certain evident advantages. They may result from democratic pressures within States, and at least they represent a voluntary commitment by individual nations to join their forces to prevent proliferation. It has been argued that the NPT is a grossly unequal Treaty:[3] but the establishment of NFZs is undoubtedly a more equitable process, seeking to secure from the nuclear powers the necessary guarantees and underpinning for the security of smaller states. The campaign for a NFZ can create a bridge between public opinion, democratic mobilization, and state initiatives. It can, in responding to a United Nations initiative, create forces which can greatly strengthen international commitment to the UN system, as a forerunner of new forms of universal co-operation.

There are two categories of involvement in nuclear-free zones. First, the states constituting any such zone need to reach an agreement about the commitments which are involved in nuclear-weapon-free status, and to resolve upon means for jointly enforcing that status. Second, the existing nuclear powers outside such a zone need to be brought to an accord which can underwrite it, by promising respect for its integrity. If the nuclear powers refuse agreement to respect the zone, then it will not succeed in establishing itself as much more than a propaganda commitment. Important though such a commitment undoubtedly is, both the First UN Special Session and the modern peace movement have expected greatly more than this. It is, of course, always possible that the nuclear powers could ratify an agreement concerning such a zone, and then violate their own obligations. This possibility raises very important problems, to the discussion of which we shall return.

With increased tensions and economic crisis, the proliferation of nuclear weapons threatens to run away without restraint. Certain "pariah" states have probably already obtained nuclear weapons, and others may be within reach of doing so.[4] Wars and revolutions beset the Third World, and encourage more and more of its statesmen to look for nuclear options. Yet, as we have already said, by far the most serious form of proliferation has been that involved in the superpower competition between the United States and the Soviet Union. Europeans in particular have reason to fear this competition, because so many of the warheads in both arsenals are both targeted upon, and based around, European cities[5]. Intense discussion has raged over a period of a decade and more, about the meaning of military doctrines of limited nuclear war, or "theatre war". It is not necessary for this argument to enter into the details of this arcane discussion. The truth is simple: no one knows how to limit a nuclear exchange once it has begun. This understanding was the basis of the convergence of the European Peace Movements at the beginning of the eighties.

Of course, everyone is aware that armament (and disarmament) is an activity of Governments, and that nothing will lift the threat of militarism if Governments do not agree. To bring them to agreement must involve a multi-national mobilisation of public opinion. In Europe, this only materialised when people appreciated the exceptional vulnerability of their continent. One prominent statesman, who both understood, and drew attention to, this extreme exposure, was Olof Palme. During a Helsinki conference of the Socialist International, he warned:

> "Europe is no special zone where peace can be taken for granted. In actual fact, it is at the centre of the arms race. Granted, the general assumption seems to be that any potential military conflict between the superpowers is going to start some place other than in Europe. But even if that were to be the case, we would have to count on one or the other party - in an effort to gain supremacy -trying to open a front on our continent, as well."[6]

Basing himself on this recognition, Mr Palme recalled various earlier attempts to create, in North and Central Europe, nuclear-free zones, from which, by agreement, all warheads were to be excluded. (We shall look at the history of these proposals below.) He then drew a conclusion of historic significance, which provides the most real, and most hopeful, possibility of generating a truly continental opposition to this continuing arms race:

"Today more than ever there is, in my opinion, every reason to go on working for a nuclear-free zone. *The ultimate objective of these efforts should be a nuclear-free Europe* (my italics)."

Olof Palme's initiative was launched exactly a month before the 1978 United Nations Special Session on Disarmament. Although the goal of the UN Special Session was "general and complete disarmament", as it should have been, it is commonly not understood that this goal was deliberately coupled with a whole series of intermediate objectives, including the steps proposed by Palme himself.

We have already cited Article 33 of the Final Statement, endorsing the goal of Nuclear-Free Zones. Later, the declaration goes on to spell out this commitment in considerable detail.

Article 63 of this final document schedules several areas for consideration as nuclear-free zones. They include Africa, where the Organisation of African Unity has resolved upon "the denuclearisation of the region", but also the Middle East and South Asia, which are listed alongside South and Central America, whose pioneering treaty offers a possible model for others to follow. This is the only populous area to have been covered by an existing agreement, which was concluded in the Treaty of Tlatelolco (a suburb of Mexico City), opened for signature from February 1967.

There are other zones which are covered by more or less similar agreements. Conservationists will be pleased that they include Antarctica, the Moon, outer space, and the seabed. Two snags exist in this respect. One is that the effectiveness of the agreed arrangements is often questioned. The other is that if civilisation is destroyed, the survivors may not be equipped to establish themselves comfortably in safe havens among penguins or deep-sea plants and fish.

leave alone upon the Moon.

Nuclear-free Zones in Europe

If Europe as a whole was late to raise the issue of its possible denuclearisation, there have been a number of efforts to sanitise smaller regions within the continent.

The idea that groups of nations in particular areas might agree to forgo the manufacture or deployment of nuclear weapons, and to eschew research into their production, was first seriously mooted in the second half of the 1950s. In 1956, the USSR attempted to open discussion on the possible restriction of armaments, under inspection, and the prohibition of nuclear weapons within both German states and some adjacent countries. The proposal was discussed in the Disarmament Sub-Committee of the United Nations, but it got no further. But afterwards the Foreign Secretary of Poland, Adam Rapacki, took to the Twelfth Session of the UN General Assembly a plan to outlaw both the manufacture and the harbouring of nuclear arsenals in all the territories of Poland, Czechoslovakia, the German Democratic Republic and the Federal German Republic. The Czechoslovaks and East Germans quickly endorsed this suggestion.

Rapacki's proposals would have come into force by four separate unilateral decisions of each relevant government. Enforcement would have been supervised by a commission drawn from NATO countries, Warsaw Pact adherents, and non-aligned states. Inspection posts, with a system of ground and air controls, were to be established to enable the commission to function. Subject to this supervision, neither nuclear weapons, nor installations capable of harbouring or servicing them, nor missile sites, would have been permitted in the entire designated area. Nuclear powers were thereupon expected to agree not to use nuclear weapons against the denuclearized zone, and not to deploy their own atomic warheads with any of their conventional forces stationed within it.

The plan was rejected by the NATO powers, on the grounds, first, that it did nothing to secure German reunification and, second, that it failed to cover the deployment of conventional armaments. In 1958, therefore, Rapacki returned with modified proposals. Now he suggested a phased approach. In the beginning, nuclear stockpiles would be frozen at their existing levels within the zone. Later, the removal of these weapon stocks would be accompanied by controlled and mutually agreed reductions in conventional forces. This initiative, too, was rejected.

Not everyone in NATO, however, approved of this rejection. Denis Healey, the Labour Party's spokesman on Foreign Affairs, gave strong support to the Polish proposal:

> "So long as Germany remains divided, a final solution of the Berlin problem is impossible. No temporary agreement on Berlin is likely to last, unless it is linked with an agreement between NATO and the Warsaw Pact to seek security by cooperation on arms control in Central Europe on both sides of the dividing line. Moreover, there is no other way of ensuring that neither part of a divided Germany obtains atomic weapons. I welcome the Polish Government's new pressure for the Rapacki plan and hope both the Soviet and Western Governments will now give it a high priority in their current discussions".[7]

So, too, from the other side of the British debate on nuclear weapons, did Bertrand Russell:

> "From the point of view of world peace, this is a wholly admirable suggestion, and it is much to be wished that the Western Powers would take it up, but I am afraid that there is little hope of their doing so. It is vehemently opposed by Adenauer, who wants a strong military Germany. It is also opposed by America, Britain, and

France, who want German armed assistance in resisting Russia. Nobody in the West seems to have noticed that the Rapacki Plan involves the disarmament of several Communist Powers, which would be an adequate counter-poise to the disarmament of Western Germany. The reliance on Western Germany by the Western Powers has dangerous aspects which are carefully ignored. German troops are still commanded by generals, many of whom are ex-Nazis. German revival under Hitler might well be a precedent. There are German troops stationed in Britain at the invitation of the British Government. It is surprising that what we all felt in 1940 can be so quickly forgotten.

"All these tangled problems would become immeasurably easier to solve if the world were to adopt Khrushchev's proposal of general and complete disarmament, which, throughout the present crisis, he has frequently renewed. What makes the Rapacki plan unacceptable to Germans is the fact that under it Germany and no other Great Power would be disarmed. If disarmament were general, this objection would lose its force."[8]

Although Rapacki's proposals impressed the oppositions, Governments in the West remained largely deaf.

Meantime, in 1957, Romania proposed a similar project to denuclearise the Balkans. This plan was reiterated in 1968, and again in 1972.

In 1959, the Irish government outlined a plan for the creation of nuclear-free zones throughout the entire planet, which were to be developed region by region. In the same year the Chinese People's Republic suggested that the Pacific Ocean and all Asia be constituted a nuclear-free zone, and in 1960 various African states elaborated similar proposals for an All-African agreement. (These were re-tabled in 1965, and yet again in 1974.)

In 1962 the Polish government offered yet another variation on the Rapacki Plan, which would have maintained its later notion of phasing, but which would now have permitted other European nations to join in if they wished to extend the original designated area. In the first stage, existing levels of nuclear weaponry and rocketry would be frozen, prohibiting the creation of new bases. Then, as in the earlier version, nuclear and conventional armaments would be progressively reduced according to a negotiated timetable. The rejection of this 1962 version was the end of the Rapacki proposals, but they were followed in 1964 by the so-called "Gomulka" plan, which was designed to affect the same area, but which offered more restricted goals.

Although the main NATO powers displayed no real interest in any of these efforts, they did arouse some real concern and sympathy in Scandinavia. As early as October 1961, the Swedish government tabled what became known as the Undén Plan (named after Sweden's Foreign Minister) at the First Committee of the UN General Assembly. This supported the idea of nuclear-free zones and a "non-atomic club",[9] and advocated their general acceptance. Certain of its proposals, concerning non-proliferation and testing, were adopted by the General Assembly. But the Undén Plan was never realised, because the USA and others maintained at the time that nuclear-free zones were an inappropriate approach to disarmament, which could only be agreed in a comprehensive "general and complete" decision. Over and again this most desirable end has been invoked to block any less total approach to discovering any practicable means by which it might be achieved.

In 1963, President Kekkonen of Finland called for the re-opening of talks on the Undén Plan. Finland and Sweden were both neutral already, he said, while Denmark and Norway, notwithstanding their membership of NATO, had no nuclear weapons of their own, and deployed none of those belonging to their Alliance. But although this constituted a *de facto* commitment, it would, he held, be notably reinforced by a deliberate collective decision to confirm it as an enduring joint policy.

The Norwegian premier responded to this *démarche* by calling for the inclusion of sections of the USSR in the suggested area. As long ago as 1959, Nikita Khrushchev had suggested a Nordic nuclear-free zone, but no approach was apparently made to him during 1963 to discover whether the USSR would be willing to underpin such a project with any concession to the Norwegian viewpoint. However, while this argument was unfolding again in 1963, Khrushchev launched yet another similar proposal, for a nuclear-free Mediterranean.

The fall of Khrushchev took much of the steam out of such diplomatic forays, even though new proposals continue to emerge at intervals. In May 1974, the Indian government detonated what it described as a "peaceful" nuclear explosion. This provoked renewed proposals for a nuclear-free zone in the Near East, from both Iran and the United Arab Republic, and it revived African concern with the problem. Probably the reverberations of the Indian bang were heard in New Zealand, because that nation offered up its first suggestion for a South Pacific free zone later in the year.

In 1975, the Conference of the Committee on Disarmament, in Geneva, set up an ad hoc group to study and report on the idea of Nuclear-free Zones. This published a *Comprehensive Study*, which was later referred to the United Nations General Assembly, and adopted that same year by a vote of 82 to 10. Seven non-aligned states sponsored this move, which also had Chinese support. Of the nuclear powers, Britain, France and the USA opposed the motion, and the Soviet Union abstained. Thus the recognition of NFZs by the United Nations was a victory for the non-aligned states. Nine NATO states voted against, and ten states (including the Ukraine and Byelorussia, Cuba and Mongolia) which were allied with the USSR, abstained.

The text of the resolution read:

> "A "nuclear weapon-free zone" shall, as a general rule, be deemed to be any zone, recognized as such by the United Nations General Assembly, which any group of states, in the free exercise of their sovereignty, has established by virtue of a treaty or convention whereby: (a) the statute of total absence of nuclear weapons to which the zone shall be subject, including the procedure for the delimitation of the zone, is defined: and (b) an international system of verification and control is established to guarantee compliance with the obligations deriving from that statute.
>
> In every case of a nuclear weapon-free zone that has been recognized as such by the General Assembly, all nuclear weapon states shall undertake or reaffirm, in a solemn international instrument having full legally binding force, such as a treaty, a convention or a protocol, the following obligations: (a) to respect in all its parts the statute of total absence of nuclear weapons defined in the treaty or convention which serves as the constitutive instrument of the zone; (b) to refrain from contributing in any way to the performance in the territories forming part of the zone of acts which involve a violation of the aforesaid treaty or convention; and (c) to refrain from using or threatening to use nuclear weapons against the states included in the zone.
>
> The above definitions in no way impair the resolutions which the General Assembly has adopted or may adopt with regard to specific cases of nuclear weapon-free zones nor the rights emanating for the member states from such resolutions."[10]

As a subsequent UN publication reported:

> "The views expressed in the general debate underlined the divergence of positions on several issues in the study, in particular with regard to the definition of the zones and the obligations of nuclear-weapon States. The Soviet Union, for instance, indicated that it was not in a position automatically to give consent to obligations with regard to a nuclear-weapon-free zone contained in a treaty on the creation of a zone. The United States objected to the implications of the draft resolution, in particular with regard to the role and competence of the General Assembly. For the United States, the General Assembly could contribute to the establishment of a zone by providing a forum for consultations and encouraging States to work towards specific arrangements. The views expressed by the United States were supported by several Western countries

which voted against the resolution. Other countries welcomed the study which, in their view, contained useful guidelines for the establishment of nuclear-weapon-free zones."[11]

During these years the European disarmament lobbies were stalemated.

But the Latin American Treaty, which is briefly discussed above, had already been concluded in 1967, and within a decade it had secured the adherence of 25 states. The last of the main nuclear powers to endorse it was the USSR, which confirmed its general support in 1978. (Cuba withholds endorsement because it reserves its rights pending the evacuation of the Guantanamo base by the United States.) African pressures for a similar agreement are, as we have already argued, notably influenced by the threat of a South African nuclear military capacity, which is an obvious menace to neighbouring Mozambique, Zimbabwe, and Angola, and a standing threat to the Organisation of African Unity. In the Middle East, Israel plays a similar catalysing role, and fear of an Israeli bomb is widespread throughout the region.

Why then, this lag between Europe and the other continents? If the pressure for denuclearised zones began in Europe, and if the need for them, as we have seen, remains direst there, why have the Governments of the Third World been, up to now, so much more effectively vocal on this issue than those of the European continent? Part of the answer surely lies in the prevalence of the non-aligned movement among the countries of the Third World. Apart from a thin scatter of neutrals, Europe is the seed-bed of alignments, and the interests of the blocs as apparently disembodied entities are commonly prayed as absolute within it.

The Modalities of NFZs

(1) The Agreement Between Members of a Nuclear-free Zone

Obviously every state which seeks the establishment of a nuclear-free zone is seeking to share in an agreement prohibiting the ownership, construction, acquisition, or use of nuclear weapons. Such an agreement may find problems of definition in determining what constitutes a nuclear weapon. Do "nuclear weapons" mean weapons employing nuclear explosives, or can they include weapons deriving their propulsion from nuclear fuels? Let us assume that this argument can be resolved: then we immediately require a whole series of definitions to control the meaning of other terms of the agreement. What is "ownership"? What is "construction"? "Acquisition"? Even, "use"?

Of course the possession of nuclear weapons can involve a variety of real situations. Some states own their own weapons, while others have developed a number of different relationships promoting the deployment of weapons belonging to others. The treaty for a nuclear-free zone will need to cast its net wide enough to forbid all of them equally. Weapons deployed directly or indirectly on behalf of a third party are, for the purposes of such an agreement, perhaps even worse than weapons directly owned and completely controlled by the party concerned. Each link in the deployment chain is liable to give rise to an uncertainty about use. A nuclear-free zone will obviously prohibit the placement of nuclear weapons in its agreed area, but most participants would presumably seek also to prohibit their co-signatories from owning and deploying such weapons in territories outside the agreed boundaries of the zone. Although this reservation seems far-fetched, there are several practical cases in which it is immediately relevant.

For example, some countries straddle boundaries. Turkey, for instance, is one. If Turkey were to seek to become a member of a European nuclear-free zone, would Turkish territory in Asia Minor be included? If it were not, consenting parties to the treaty inside Europe could imaginably be bombarded by Turkish-based nuclear weapons held outside the agreed boundaries of the zone. It seems fairly clear that no state could be allowed to occupy a schizoid position of this kind. The example of Turkey is not the only one in this category, and that is why the Soviet Union cannot simultaneously place part of its territory in, and part outside, a nuclear-free zone. This fact, not any lack of sensitivity to the "European" status of Russia, persuades many advocates of European Nuclear Disarmament of the advantage of the slogan of a "Europe free of nuclear weapons, from Poland to Portugal" rather than "from the Atlantic to the Urals".

A nuclear-free zone treaty would also have to define manufacture or construction in a clear and precise way. Every nuclear reactor is a potential hazard in this respect. If British nuclear power stations are supplying plutonium for the American nuclear weapons programme, then surely they are helping the "manufacture" of nuclear weapons. The British authorities deny such co-operation, saying that the plutonium which they supply to the United States goes there for civilian purposes only. But if the civilian use of British plutonium liberates American produced plutonium for the American military programme, is this not a specious quibble? States consenting to join a nuclear-free zone may wish to elaborate a framework which could clarify policy about such matters.

Let us assume that precise definitions of all these terms can be agreed. No signatory will make nuclear weapons or conduce to their manufacture, either on their own behalf, or in co-operation with any third party; no signatory will allow deployment of nuclear warheads or any other nuclear explosive machines, either on their own behalf or in co-operation with any third party; and no signatory will permit the transportation of nuclear weapons over their territory, including their territorial waters and their national air space.

It would be both reasonable and simple for the parties consenting to such a treaty to further pledge themselves to refrain from testing nuclear devices outside the territorial area covered by the treaty agreement.

Although it would not be by any means useless for existing non-nuclear powers to league themselves into nuclear-free zones, we may assume that some nuclear-free zones in Europe would be likely to include states which are at present deploying nuclear weapons of one kind or another within their national territories. If we could suppose that say, Austria, Switzerland and Yugoslavia were able to establish a nuclear-free zone treaty, this would undoubtedly exercise some persuasive influence in the other parts of Europe which are less fortunate in that their territories are already defiled by the presence of nuclear weapons. But if there is an agreement in the Central European zone or in the Balkans, either case will involve the physical withdrawal of any nuclear weapons which may be presently emplaced. Rather precise arrangements will be necessary to determine such withdrawal.

At the same time, members of a nuclear-free zone will need to decide how far they wish to extend their prohibitions to cover equipment which is ancillary to the deployment of nuclear weapons. Should launchers and other emplacements also be specifically forbidden within the agreed territory? It would seem so.

(2) The Underwriting of Nuclear-free Zones by the Nuclear Powers

Naturally, nuclear-free zones offer but the sparsest imitation of security if they are not recognised by the existing nuclear powers and if those powers do not give solemn undertakings to respect their status.

In the case of the Treaty of Tlatelolco, there are two protocols which have been endorsed by the nuclear powers, respecting and accepting the agreement that nuclear weapons may not be deployed within the Treaty area. The second protocol, for instance, agrees to fully respect the Treaty, and to refrain from violating it. It further commits its signatories not to use or threaten to use nuclear weapons against the contracting parties of the main Treaty.

Many people have questioned whether the Latin American Treaty goes far enough in the requirements it imposes on the nuclear powers. Should not those powers agree to prohibit the sale of nuclear materials which could be used for military purposes? Should they not agree to disconnect any linkages with nuclear weapons aspects of any existing military alliances? But undoubtedly the major problem about nuclear power recognition of nuclear-free zones is that of enforcement. To this we shall return later.

(3) The Development of Nuclear-free Zones in Europe

The two sub-regions of Europe which have made most progress towards the development of nuclear-free zones are the Northern (Nordic) area and the

Balkan zone. A recent conference in Athens brought together representatives from Romania, Bulgaria, Yugoslavia and Turkey, at the invitation of the Greek Government which hosted the meeting. Interestingly, there was a parallel conference involving some of the peace movements of Europe. Although this failed to agree a communique, it afforded useful opportunities for discussion.

The conference was preceded by a joint appeal against the deployment of nuclear missiles in Europe, launched by President Ceausescu of Romania and Andreas Papandreou, the Greek Prime Minister. In a letter to Presidents Reagan and Andropov the two European leaders opposed the deployment of intermediate range nuclear missiles in Europe, to the considerable annoyance of some client states such as Great Britain. (The Greek Ambassador in London was informed by the Foreign Office that it was "extremely annoyed" that Greece had failed to consult Britain before joining in so unusual a declaration.)

The Athens conference began after a two week delay, whilst the Turkish Government manoeuvred about whether to join or not. The Romanians in particular reasonably insisted that a Balkan meeting needed Turkish representation, although the Turks were, at best, lukewarm about the proposal. From the beginning they made it clear that they did not believe that the Balkans could be separated from the rest of Europe on matters of nuclear weapons. However, they were anxious to be present in any multilateral gathering of Balkan states, and they agreed to attend provided the de-nuclearisation plan was placed last on an agenda of five points. Surprisingly, very prompt agreement was reached among the other states to accept this proviso.

However, the Turks were not mollified by this, and when the talks took place, they maintained the unconstructive view that "the right forum for discussing nuclear weapons control is the US-Soviet talks in Geneva, not somewhere on the periphery". Greece and Turkey are the only Balkan nations harbouring nuclear weapons, so clearly it is necessary to try to secure Turkish agreement to the creation of a nuclear-free zone. Paradoxically, both Greece and Turkey are harbouring American nuclear weapons, even though mutual suspicions ensure the most uneasy of relationships between them. It is arguable that the conflict between Greece and Turkey is perhaps the most intransigent of all the national rivalries on the European mainland, and it is instructive that this fracture exists within one of the alliances, not across the divide of the cold war.

The commitment of the Greeks to a nuclear-free zone is evident, and is made plain in the fact that it was their initiative to convene the February 1984 conference. They have sought to maintain the momentum of this initiative in a series of subsequent meetings. Bulgaria and Romania have also declared in favour of a nuclear-free zone, as has Yugoslavia. However, the Yugoslavs could reasonably insist that such a zone, constituted in a region so sensitive to superpower confrontations, would be meaningless without fully adequate guarantees from the United States and the Soviet Union. The Athens diplomatic conference ended with a cautious statement, promising to continue discussions.

The problem of securing compliance from the superpowers is, of course, to put it very mildly, no less intractable than that of reconciling the conflicting interests of Greece and Turkey. The United States has expressed strong opposition to the Balkan nuclear-free zone on the grounds that it would alter the strategic balances in the Eastern Mediterranean, without securing adequate concessions from the Soviet Union. The claim is that Warsaw Treaty armed forces are superior in conventional weaponry and that the Turkish and Greek nuclear weapons provide a necessary rung in the ladder of "deterrent" forces. Many authorities have argued against this point of view elsewhere, and it is hardly necessary to repeat those arguments here. But there is a problem not only between, but also *within* the alliances. A non-nuclear Greece, for instance, might be rather apprehensive about a Turkey which deployed an extensive nuclear arsenal, even if it were under American control.

More seriously, since the deployment of Soviet intermediate range missiles in the German Democratic Republic and Czechoslovakia, it was argued by some independent scholars as well as Western specialists that the "neutralisation" of South Eastern Europe disproportionately weakens NATO's Southern flank. If the American presence were to be reduced or removed from this zone, such people have argued that Soviet pressures could easily increase, not only on Greece and Turkey, but also on Yugoslavia. Clearly, the reciprocal Central European deployments hindered progress in the Balkans.

The heightened nuclear face-off between the two Germanies and in Central Europe was also an undoubted set-back to the progress of the Nordic nuclear-free zone. In the epoch of Mikhail Gorbachev's moratorium on tests, however, the Soviet Union has seized the initiative on disarmament questions, and there have arisen new possibilities in the Northern area. Both in the North and South of Europe the conclusion of the treaty on the destruction of Intermediate Nuclear Forces opens out opportunities for progress.

By contrast with the Balkan area, none of the Nordic states harbours nuclear weapons, and all have signed the non-proliferation treaty. Finland and Sweden are committed neutrals, and the Swedes have a consistent policy of "non-alignment in peace aiming at neutrality in war". Denmark, Norway and Iceland are aligned in NATO, but both the Danes and the Norwegians have declared that they will not allow nuclear weapons to be stationed on their territories during peacetime. In one sense, then, there is already an embryonic nuclear-free zone in Northern Europe. However, the separate commitments of the different states of the region do not have the benefit of underpinning by reciprocal commitments on the part of the nuclear powers. The quickest progress towards this would probably come from the formal conclusion of a treaty in the area which would leave nuclear powers caught in the crossfire of world public opinion.

Within the language of "mutual and balanced force reductions", it would be impossible for either superpower to justify heightened escalation in the central zone of Europe whilst both were moving to disengagement in the North and South. But it will not, long term, be sufficient for one superpower to sponsor the proposed lesser nuclear-free zones and underwrite them alone. This fact will be a brake on development unless there arises a real possibility of loosening up within one or another, if not both, alliance systems. For this reason, the campaign against the deployment of intermediate-range missiles across Europe maintained a vital importance. Its success, in the INF Treaty, should not lead to any relaxation of effort.

In central Europe, the remarkable agreements between the Socialist Party in West Germany, and the governing Party in the East, indicate that such efforts remain entirely worthwhile. From the point of view of the peace movements, to be sure, the triumph of a small nuclear-free zone on any sector of the dividing line between the blocs would be an important breakthrough. It is increasingly difficult to see any likely circumstances in which a single agreement could embrace the whole of Europe at one sweep: all the tangible progress towards discussion between Governments has so far taken place on a much smaller scale. Yet, even if the sometimes large obstacles to practical agreement in either the Balkan or Nordic regions could all be overcome there would remain a vast problem for the realisation of a comprehensive European solution. Smaller nuclear-free zones will meet with the same difficulties as larger ones, and foremost amongst these is the question of enforcement.

(4) Enforcement

The enforcement of a nuclear-free zone may not be easy for the individual consenting states within it. It is presumably possible for them to reach agreement about their own conduct, and any mechanisms for inspection and control which may be necessary. There exists an international body which is charged with controlling nuclear materials: the International Atomic Energy Agency. This Agency does not command universal support, and has been open to various criticisms.[12] There seems to be no special reason why the IAEA should be the monopoly custodian of inspectors' powers within nuclear-free zones. The Treaty of Tlatelolco has an enforcement committee. It would be possible for new treaties to agree open inspection mechanisms which were as rigorous as their consenting parties felt to be desirable. However, whilst internal inspection by agreement is simple in principle, enforcement by observance on the outside nuclear powers is far more difficult. When nuclear powers feel their interests to be in jeopardy, they have already shown themselves to be less than scrupulous about the observance of international treaties. None of the wars which have plagued humanity during this century would have been possible if all the powers involved in them had respected all the treaty undertakings they had ever signed. More: there is some evidence that the Latin American treaty has already been breached by at least one, maybe two, nuclear powers. There is much diplomatic work to do, in order to develop even the Latin American prototype of a nuclear-free zone so that it could operate in more contentious regions. But what happens when inspection reveals that it is a nuclear power which is acting in violation of non-nuclear agreements? The latest evidence on this score is provided in a related sphere: the United States' Government is credibly accused of mining Nicaraguan territorial waters, and causing damage both to Soviet and Japanese ships, amongst others. Clamorous evidence is offered by American politicians to the effect that mines have been directly placed by the Central Intelligence Agency. The refusal of the United States' Government to answer Nicaraguan complaints to the World Court, and its declared intention of ignoring any relevant proceedings of that Court for a period of two years, show us some of the limits of international law, when we confront such crucial issues as nuclear disarmament.[13] How may the weak compel the strong? It seems transparently plain that institutions for reaching public opinion are more important than institutions of force, if this task is not to be rendered totally futile.

(5) The Role of the Peace Movements in Resisting Proliferation

Links between peace movements have been the first stage in diagnosing this problem. Already the Japanese Council Against A and H Bombs has pioneered international contact on the widest scale and reached out to form links with the growing campaign for European Nuclear Disarmament.

In Europe, successive Conventions of the main peace movements in Western and neutral states have established a continuing dialogue between the main organisations in the field. The first Convention, in Brussels, in 1982, was fortunate in having the presence of the Venerable Gyotsu Sato, who established close contacts with many of the most important organisations. Strong European representation resulted at the World Conference Against A and H Bombs in Tokyo in 1982, and again in 1983. A powerful delegation from Japan also attended the second European Nuclear Disarmament Convention which was held in Berlin in 1983. By the time of the Perugia Convention in 1984 there had been an unfortunate split in the Japanese movement, but there were still important contacts with Pacific regional movements, which were also represented at the later Conventions in Amsterdam and Evry (near Paris) during 1985 and 1986. Beginning at Perugia, Chinese participation also widened the possibility of dialogue in all the succeeding European Conventions. At the Coventry Convention, in 1987, there began a very open and serious dialogue with the Soviet Peace Committee, and the Hungarian Peace Committee was the first East European organisation with official recognition to adhere to the European co-ordination involved in planning these meetings.

The growth of these contacts is of extraordinary importance. More and more American peace movements are relating to the initiatives of both European and Pacific peace activists. If there is one further task which now presses all of the peace movements, it is this: in a number of continental areas, the debate on the threat of nuclear war lags far behind the level already reached in the European and Pacific "theatres". Together, it is surely necessary for such movements to consider how to encourage that debate, and how to widen the circle of contacts, in order to create a veritable unity of all the peoples, able to defend all real steps towards disarmament, and to oppose any regression, no matter by whom. The forums of peace movements, both in the Pacific and in Europe, understand the need for a policy of strict non-alignment. Paradoxically, peace movements are less organized and less extensive in many of the areas where the movement of non-aligned states is strongest. Generally it is these states which suffer most from the bad behaviour of nuclear powers. Somehow, surely their peoples must find a way to join their forces to these questions?

Appendix
Restrictions on Nuclear Weapons: Treaties in Force

There follows an official United Nations Summary of the existing agreements prohibiting nuclear weapons in certain areas and nations.

International agreements to ensure the absence of nuclear weapons in certain areas and environments include the following: the Antarctic Treaty (1959); Treaty for the Prohibition of Nuclear Weapons in Latin America (1967); and the Treaty on the Prohibition of the Emplacement of Nuclear Weapons and Other Weapons of Mass Destruction on the Sea-Bed and the Ocean Floor and in the Subsoil Thereof (1971). In addition, nuclear weapons are excluded from outer space, the Moon and other celestial bodies.

A. THE ANTARCTIC TREATY

The Antarctic Treaty, concluded on 1 December 1959, was the first international agreement which, by establishing a demilitarized zone, *ipso facto* ensured that nuclear weapons would not be introduced into a specified area.

The Treaty, which basically establishes that Antarctica is to be used for peaceful purposes only, was not intended to solve the problem of different territorial claims, but rather to ensure access to the whole of the area in order to carry out scientific research and to prevent it from becoming "the scene or object of international discord".

Article V of the Treaty specifically prohibits nuclear explosions and the disposal of radioactive waste material in Antarctica. It does not rule out those activities for peaceful purposes indefinitely but makes them subject to future international agreements on the question.

The prohibition against the introduction and testing of nuclear weapons falls within the scope of article 1 of the Treaty, which bans "any measures of a military nature" such as the establishment of military bases and fortifications, military manoeuvres and the testing of any type of weapon. It does not, however, prevent the use of military personnel and equipment for scientific research and other peaceful purposes.

Under the Treaty's system of verification, observers appointed by each of the original contracting parties have the right of aerial observation and of complete access at all times to any area or installation.

The regime established by the Treaty has been scrupulously observed. This is reflected in the fact that no violations have been reported since it came into force and there has been no indication that any problems have arisen with regard to its verification.

The Treaty entered into force on 23 June 1961 and the number of parties to it has increased from the original 12 signatories in 1959 to 32 as of the end of 1984.

The question of Antarctica was raised anew in 1983 in the General Assembly. At the initiative of Malaysia, and with support from mostly non-aligned States, the Assembly adopted a resolution by which, *inter alia*, it requested the Secretary-General to prepare a comprehensive factual and objective study on all aspects of Antarctica, taking into account the Treaty as well as other relevant factors. The study, submitted to the 1984 session of the General Assembly, deals with the legal and political aspects, scientific research and natural resources in Antarctica, and also contains the views of 54 States on the issue. During the debate, Malaysia indicated that it would not at that time press its proposal for the establishment of a United Nations committee on Antarctica, but it insisted that any arrangements concerning that region's resources should be freely negotiated and concluded in a forum authorized or organized by the United Nations.

B. TREATY FOR THE PROHIBITION OF NUCLEAR WEAPONS IN LATIN AMERICA

The Treaty for the Prohibition of Nuclear Weapons in Latin America (Treaty of Tlatelolco) was the first Treaty to establish a nuclear-weapon-free zone in a densely populated area. It was also the first agreement to establish a system of international control and a permanent supervisory organ, the Agency for the Prohibition of Nuclear Weapons in Latin America (OPANAL).

Meeting in Mexico City in November 1964, 17 Latin American countries set up a preparatory commission to draw up a preliminary text for a denuclearization treaty, defining obligations and a system of control. After two years of negotiations, the Treaty was signed on 14 February 1967, at Tlatelolco, a borough of Mexico City, and was endorsed by the General Assembly later the same year.

The basic obligation of the parties to the Treaty, defined in article 1, is to use exclusively for peaceful purposes the nuclear material and facilities under their jurisdiction, and to prohibit and prevent in their respective territories the very presence of nuclear weapons for any purpose and under any circumstances.

Parties to the Treaty also undertake to refrain from engaging in, encouraging or authorizing, directly or indirectly, or in any way participating in the testing, use, manufacture, production, possession or control of any nuclear weapon.

OPANAL was set up in June 1969. Its control system includes safeguards to be negotiated with IAEA with respect to all the nuclear activities of the parties.

Annexed to the Treaty are two Additional Protocols which create a system of obligations for extra-continental and continental States having responsibility *de jure* or *de facto* for territories in the zone of application of the Treaty and for the nuclear-weapon States.

Thus, under Additional Protocol I, France, the Netherlands, the United Kingdom and the United States would agree to guarantee nuclear-weapon-free status to those territories for which they are, *de jure* or *de facto*, internationally responsible. The Protocol has been signed and ratified by the Netherlands, the United Kingdom and the United States. France has signed it and has declared that it will in due course take an appropriate decision.

Under Additional Protocol II, nuclear-weapon States pledge to respect fully the "denuclearization of Latin America in respect of warlike purposes" and "not to use or threaten to use nuclear weapons against the Contracting Parties". By 1979, all five nuclear-weapon States had adhered to it.

As of 31 December 1987, the Treaty had been ratified by 25 eligible States and was in force for the 23 States which had waived the requirement for entry into force that all States in the zone be parties to the Treaty, that all States to which the Protocols apply adhere to them and that relevant safeguards agreements be concluded with IAEA.

C. SEA-BED TREATY

In the late 1960s, with marked advances in the

science of oceanography and the growing interest of all nations in the potential resources available in the sea, the General Assembly became increasingly concerned with the need for an international régime to govern the uses of the sea-bed and ocean floor beyond territorial waters. In 1967, on the initiative of Malta, the Assembly discussed the question of reserving that area exclusively for peaceful purposes and exploiting its resources for the benefit of mankind. Special concern was expressed that it be done without impairment of a marine environment. The Assembly, therefore, established a sea-bed committee to deal with these matters.

The question of the regulation of the uses of the sea-bed was also discussed at length in the Eighteen Nation Committee on Disarmament (ENDC), from 1968 until the end of 1970. In a memorandum submitted in 1968, the Soviet Union proposed that there be an international agreement on limiting the military use of the sea-bed and ocean floor and, in particular, banning the establishment of fixed military installations. At the same time, the President of the United States, in a message to the ENDC, called on that body to begin negotiations on an agreement "which would prohibit the use of the new environment for the emplacement of weapons of mass destruction".

In 1969, the Soviet Union and the United States submitted a joint draft treaty to the ENDC. After intensive consideration in various bodies, a revised draft treaty was submitted to the General Assembly. The final draft was approved by a vote of 104 to 2 (El Salvador and Peru), with 2 abstentions (Ecuador and France), on 7 December 1970.

The Treaty provides that the States Parties to it undertake not to place on or under the sea-bed, beyond the outer limit of a 12-mile coastal zone, any nuclear weapons or any other weapons of mass destruction or any facilities for such weapons. Each State Party "shall have the right to verify through observation the activities of other States Parties" provided that "observation does not interfere with such activities". If one Party doubts another's compliance with its obligations under the Treaty, the two Parties are to hold consultations. If reasonable doubts persist, "the State Party having such doubts shall notify the other States Parties, and the Parties concerned shall co-operate on such further procedures for verification as may be agreed, including appropriate inspection of objects, structures, installations or other facilities". If consultation and co-operation do not remove the doubts concerning the fulfilment of the obligations assumed under the Treaty, a State Party may, in accordance with the provisions of the United Nations Charter, refer the matter to the Security Council.

The Treaty was opened for signature on 11 February 1971. It entered into force on 18 May 1972. By the end of 1987, 77 States had become parties to the Treaty.

Two Review Conferences of the Parties to the Treaty were held, in 1977 and 1983, to determine if the provisions of the Treaty were being realized (article VII). In the Final Declarations of both Review Conferences, the State Parties confirmed that the obligations assumed under article 1 of the Treaty had been faithfully observed. While making a favourable assessment of the effectiveness of the Treaty since 1972, they also recognized that it should be supplemented by additional measures to exclude the sea-bed area from the arms race. Accordingly, they suggested that the Conference on Disarmament consider the matter further, in consultation with the States Parties to the Treaty. During its 1985 session, the Conference expressed the view, *inter alia*, that the scope of the sea-bed Treaty should be broadened, that its provisions governing procedures for verification and compliance should be improved and that access to information on relevant technological developments should be facilitated.

D. OUTER SPACE TREATY

The Treaty on Principles Governing the Activities of States in the Exploration and Use of Outer Space, including the Moon and Other Celestial Bodies was concluded in 1967 in order to ensure that the environment would be used for the benefit of all peoples.

E. SOUTH PACIFIC TREATY

The South Pacific Nuclear Free Zone Treaty (Treaty of Rarotonga) was opened for signature on 6 August 1985, and entered into force on 11 December 1986. Nine members of the South Pacific Forum had ratified the Treaty as of 31 July 1987.

The Treaty establishes a very large nuclear-free zone in the South Pacific. It stretches from the west of Australia to the boundary of the Latin American nuclear-weapon-free zone on the east, and it extends from the Equator to the boundary of the Antarctica demilitarized zone on the south.

The authors of the Treaty recognized, however, that the parties to the Treaty could be responsible only for actions regarding their own ships and aircraft; consequently, nothing in the Treaty affects the exercise of the rights of any State under international law with regard to freedom of the seas.

Each party to the Treaty undertakes not to manufacture, acquire, possess or have control over any nuclear explosive device inside or outside the zone. Moreover, it undertakes to conduct any nuclear activities in co-operation with other States in accordance with strict non-proliferation measures to provide assurance of exclusively peaceful non-exclusive use, and to support the effectiveness of the international non-proliferation system based on the non-proliferation Treaty and the safeguards system of the International Atomic Energy Agency.

While exercising its sovereign rights to decide for itself whether to allow foreign ships (which may be nuclear powered or nuclear-armed) to visit its ports or navigate its territorial seas, or foreign aircraft to visit its airfields or fly over its airspace, each party undertakes to prevent any nuclear explosive device from being stationed in its territory. It also undertakes not to test any such device or to assist others to do so. It further undertakes not to dump radio-active wastes anywhere at sea within the zone and to prevent such dumping by anyone in its territorial sea.

The States outside the zone that have jurisdiction over territories within it (France, the United Kingdom and the United States) would, upon becoming parties to Protocol 1, apply the Treaty's key provisions to those territories. The five nuclear-weapon States would, upon becoming parties to Protocol 2, undertake not to use or threaten to use nuclear explosive devices against parties to the Treaty, and the same five States would, upon becoming parties to Protocol 3, refrain from nuclear testing within the zone.

Proposals for nuclear weapon-free zones
Proposals for nuclear-weapon-free zones in several regions of the world have been discussed in the General Assembly and elsewhere for almost three decades. They have concerned such geographic areas as Africa, the Balkans, Central Europe, the

Mediterranean, the Middle East, Northern Europe, South Africa and the South Pacific.

A. AFRICA

The interest of African countries in establishing a nuclear-weapon-free zone in their continent was first expressed in the early 1960s. Initially, their attention focused on obtaining agreement that the territory of Africa should not be used for nuclear test explosions and was related to the plans of France to carry out a series of tests in the Sahara. In this connection, the General Assembly in 1961, acting on a proposal of 14 African States, called on Member States not to carry out nuclear tests in Africa in any form, to refrain from using Africa for storing or transporting nuclear weapons and to respect the continent as a nuclear-weapon-free zone. The resolution was adopted by a vote of 55 to none, with 44 abstentions.

Later on the concept was broadened. Thus, at a 1964 summit conference, the heads of State and Government of the Organization of African Unity (OAU) issued the Declaration on the Denuclearization of Africa, in which they solemnly declared their readiness to undertake, through an international agreement to be concluded under United Nations auspices, not to manufacture or control atomic weapons, and appealed to all peace-loving nations to accept the same undertaking and to all the nuclear Powers to respect the Declaration and conform to it.

Endorsing the Declaration in 1965, the General Assembly expressed the hope that African States would initiate studies to implement the denuclearization of the continent and take the necessary measures through OAU to achieve that end. It also requested the Secretary-General to extend to OAU any assistance requested for that purpose. At the same time, the Assembly called on all States not to transfer nuclear weapons, scientific data or technical assistance, either directly or indirectly, in any form that might be used to aid in the manufacture or use of nuclear weapons in Africa. The resolution was adopted by a vote of 105 to none, with 2 abstentions (France and Portugal).

Ten years after the Declaration of OAU, in 1974, the General Assembly adopted a resolution which called upon all States to consider and respect the continent of Africa as a nuclear-weapon-free zone, and every year since then, the General Assembly has adopted resolutions reiterating that appeal by the international community.

Meanwhile, grave concern has been expressed by the international community at South Africa's nuclear capability. The General Assembly, starting in 1976, in the context of its discussions on the establishment of a nuclear-weapon-free zone in Africa, has paid particular attention to developments related to activities of South Africa in the nuclear field and has adopted resolutions on the matter.

In 1979, as a result of a report indicating that a small nuclear explosion might have been conducted in the area of the Indian Ocean and the South Atlantic, the General Assembly, on the initiative of Nigeria, requested the Secretary-General to undertake a study on South Africa's plan and its capability in the nuclear field.

The Study, prepared by the Group of Experts in 1981, stated, *inter alia*, that "there is no doubt that South Africa has the technical capability to make nuclear weapons and the necessary means of delivery" and expressed the view that the introduction of nuclear weapons into the African continent, and particularly in such a volatile region as southern Africa, would not only be a severe blow to world-wide efforts at non-proliferation, but would also upset many years' efforts to spare the African continent from the nuclear arms race and to make it a nuclear-weapon-free zone. The General Assembly, for its part, has adopted resolutions on the issue in all recent years. In 1983, it requested The United Nations Institute for Disarmament Research (UNIDIR), in co-operation with the Department for Disarmament Affairs and in consultation with the OAU, to provide data on the continued development of South Africa's nuclear capability. The report was submitted to the Assembly in 1984.

The question of the nuclear capability of South Africa has been on the agenda of the Disarmament Commission since its re-establishment in 1979, following the first special session on disarmament. Due to divergent views regarding the question of possible assistance to South Africa in the nuclear field and the scope of the proposed sanctions, the Commission has been unable to agree on a text of recommendations.

B. THE BALKANS

The establishment of a nuclear-weapon-free zone in the Balkans has been the subject of several initiatives and specific proposals put forward by various States. As early as September 1957, Romania proposed the establishment of an area of peace in the Balkans free of foreign military bases. The idea was subsequently further detailed by Romania and taken up by other countries as well, including the Soviet Union. Thus, in 1959, the USSR suggested that the Balkan peninsula be made a region of peace, without any missiles or nuclear weapons. On various occasions the Balkan countries, including Albania, Bulgaria, Romania and Yugoslavia, expressed support and interest in the zone specifying at the same time some of their concerns and ideas on the modalities and scope of such a zone.

Since the beginning of the 1980s, the idea of inter-Balkan co-operation for creating a nuclear-weapon-free zone has once again become the focus of intensified public and governmental attention in most of the countries in the region. Thus, at summit meetings held in 1982, 1983 and 1984, Bulgaria, Greece, Romania and Yugoslavia supported in their joint statements and declarations the transformation of the Balkans into a nuclear-weapon-free zone, or into a zone of peace and co-operation free of nuclear weapons, and made suggestions for elaborating a nuclear-weapon-free status for the Balkans. While attaching great importance to the transformation of the Balkans into a zone of peace and co-operation free from nuclear weapons, Yugoslavia has considered that the success of such a proposal depends on the overall situation in the broader region of the Mediterranean and Europe. Turkey, for its part, in expressing its support for the concept and of zones of peace and nuclear-weapon-free zones wherever possible and feasible, has noted that the security of the Balkans is directly related to that of Europe as a whole and that one cannot be separated from the other.

At the initiative of Greece, a conference of governmental experts from Bulgaria, Greece, Romania, Turkey and Yugoslavia was held in Athens in January/February 1984 with an agenda which included the question of the establishment of a nuclear-weapon-free zone in the Balkans. It was agreed by the experts that the ideas, proposals and suggestions which were registered during the Conference would be submitted for consideration of the Governments of the participating States in order to continue the dialogue started at that

Conference. It was the first meeting in Europe of governmental experts representing States belonging to different military alliances or having non-aligned status that discussed proposals for the establishment of a nuclear-weapon-free zone in the Balkans.

C. CENTRAL EUROPE

Proposals for a nuclear-weapon-free zone in Central Europe were put forward on numerous occasions in the 1950s. In March 1956, the Soviet Union proposed in the Disarmament Commission that a zone be created in Central Europe where armaments would be subject to limitation and inspection and the stationing of any atomic or hydrogen weapons would be prohibited. Poland formally put forward in the General Assembly a proposal for a nuclear-weapon-free zone (Rapacki Plan), first in 1957 and again in 1958. The latter version provided for a nuclear-weapon-free zone covering Poland, Czechoslovakia, the Democratic Republic of Germany and the Federal Republic of Germany. According to the plan, there would be no nuclear weapons in that area; the use of such weapons against it would be forbidden and a broad system of control would be introduced.

The proposal was supported by socialist countries. Western countries, for their part, objected to it on the ground that it made no reference to limiting conventional forces and involved a variety of political and strategic problems closely related to the geographical area covered. These comments reflected differences between NATO and the parties to the Warsaw Treaty concerning major political and strategic issues such as the German problem, the military balance in Europe, the introduction of tactical and medium-range nuclear weapons and NATO's plans to create multinational nuclear forces.

In order to meet some of the Western objections, Poland submitted two more versions of the plan to the ENDC in 1962. The revisions provided, among other things, for the reduction of some conventional forces. In 1964, without withdrawing the Rapacki Plan, Poland submitted a new plan (Gomulka Plan), which did not call for an immediate reduction of the nuclear weapons already deployed within the zone, but envisaged a freeze at the existing level; in addition, an extensive system of verification was stipulated. Since then, Poland has on various occasions reaffirmed the validity of its 1957 proposal, as developed in subsequent years, as well as that of 1964.

In 1982 the Independent Commission on Disarmament and Security Issues (the Palme Commission), convinced that there must be substantial reductions in nuclear stockpiles leading to the denuclearization of Europe, recommended the establishment of a battlefield nuclear-weapon-free zone, starting with Central Europe and extending ultimately from the northern to the southern flanks of the NATO and Warsaw Treaty alliances. This scheme was to be implemented in the context of an agreement on parity and mutual force reductions in Central Europe. No nuclear munitions were to be permitted in the zone.

More recently, in 1983, the question of establishing a nuclear-weapon-free zone in Central Europe was also discussed in the Disarmament Commission. In that context, Mexico suggested that the Disarmament Commission should endorse the proposal of the Palme Commission envisaging the creation of a battlefield nuclear-weapon-free zone in Central Europe. Mexico then called on the members of the two military alliances to begin negotiations on the issue without further delay. This proposal was supported by a number of delegations, but others raised objections to it on various grounds. Due to these differences, the Disarmament Commission recommended that the proposal be duly taken into account in ongoing and future disarmament efforts.

D. MIDDLE EAST

The danger of nuclear-weapon proliferation posed by the greater access of States to nuclear technology and particularly the danger of the rapid diffusion of such technology within the political setting of the Middle East led Iran, in 1974, to ask the General Assembly to consider the question of establishing a denuclearized zone in the Middle East. Egypt subsequently co-sponsored the request.

The proposal to establish such a zone was supported by most States of the region and the first resolution on the question was adopted by the Assembly on 9 December 1974. By the resolution, the Assembly commended the idea of establishing a nuclear-weapon-free zone in the Middle East and considered that it was indispensable that all concerned parties in the area "proclaim solemnly and immediately their intention to refrain, on a reciprocal basis, from producing, testing, obtaining, acquiring or in any other way possessing nuclear weapons". It also called upon the States concerned, that had not yet done so, to accede to the non-proliferation Treaty. In pursuance of that resolution, the Secretary-General invited views and ideas from those States and subsequently submitted a report containing the responses received.

Each year between 1975 and 1984, the General Assembly has adopted resolutions on this issue. Since its 1980 session, they have been adopted by consensus.

Recently there has been increasing concern about Israel's reported nuclear-weapon capability. Thus, in 1979, the General Assembly requested the Secretary-General to undertake a study on the issue. The study, *Israeli Nuclear Armament*, submitted by the Secretary-General to the General Assembly in 1981, concluded that there was widespread agreement among technical experts that, given Israel's nuclear activities and level of expertise, it was capable of manufacturing nuclear explosive devices and possessed the means of delivery of such weapons to targets in the area, but the experts were unable to conclude definitely whether or not Israel was currently in possession of nuclear weapons. The study also stated that "the possession of nuclear weapons by Israel would be a serious destabilizing factor in the already tense situation prevailing in the Middle East, in addition to being a serious danger to the cause of non-proliferation in general".

The proposal for the creation of a nuclear-weapon-free zone in the Middle East has met with wide acceptance in the General Assembly and over a period of several years it has enjoyed wide support in the region itself.

E. MEDITERRANEAN

On 27 May 1963, the USSR submitted to the Eighteen Nations Committee on Disarmament a proposal suggesting that the whole Mediterranean area should be declared a zone free of nuclear weapons. Subsequently, the Soviet Union and the States Parties to the Warsaw Treaty have made proposals aimed at eliminating nuclear weapons from the Mediterranean. Some States bordering the Mediterranean seem to have given high priority to proposals for the establishment of nuclear-weapon-free zones in that area. Other States concerned have adopted a more general approach directed towards the transformation of the Mediterranean into a region of peace, security and co-operation, free from confrontation and conflict. Still others, such as Italy and France, have stated that security in the Mediterranean is inseparable from European security as a whole. Thus, in the view of these States, any disarmament measure envisaged for the Mediterranean should be precisely defined and cannot be undertaken in isolation from disarmament measures for all of Europe.

The various approaches are summarized in the analytical report of the Secretary-General on the strengthening of security and co-operation in the Mediterranean region, based on replies from 27 Governments, which he submitted to the General Assembly in 1983.

They are also reflected in the resolutions entitled "Strengthening of security and co-operation in the Mediterranean region", adopted without a vote by the General Assembly in 1983 and in 1984.

F. NORTHERN EUROPE

The idea of establishing a nuclear-weapon-free zone in Northern Europe was first suggested by the Soviet Union in 1958. That idea was followed up in several subsequent statements by Soviet officials indicating support for a nuclear-weapon-free zone in the Scandinavian peninsula and the Baltic area, as well as for the combining of three proposed zones -Scandinavian-Baltic, Central Europe and Balkan-Adriatic - into a single nuclear-weapon-free zone.

In the early 1960s, several suggestions were made regarding the establishment of a nuclear-weapon-free zone in the Nordic and Baltic areas. They were related in part to proposals put forward at that time for other nuclear-weapon-free zones in Europe, and in part to the consideration, in the United Nations, of the proposal submitted by Sweden (Undén Plan) for a non-nuclear club. Since 1963 the idea of establishing a nuclear-weapon-free zone in Northern Europe has been advocated most notably by Finland. It has pointed out that despite the differences in their security policies, none of the Nordic countries has acquired nuclear weapons or accepted those belonging to other States on its territory. Accordingly, a Nordic nuclear-weapon-free zone would only confirm, through mutual undertakings, the existing *de facto* situation of the absence of nuclear weapons without impairing the security of the Nordic countries or affecting the balance of power in the world (Kekkonen Plan).

The idea gained new momentum when, in 1978, Finland returned to its 1963 proposal, urging negotiations on arms regulation by the Nordic countries among themselves and together with the great Powers concerned. The objective would be a separate treaty arrangement covering the Nordic countries, which would isolate them as completely as possible from the effects of nuclear strategy in general and from nuclear weapons technology in particular. The Finnish Government has several times reiterated its position on this issue, notably in May 1983, when it stated that the idea had lost none of its validity and that Finland would continue to work for its realization. The different attitudes of the Nordic Governments have prevented the achievement of concrete results thus far. However, their foreign ministers have since 1981 discussed the question in their regular meetings.

The Soviet Union has on various occasions expressed an active interest in the establishment of the nuclear-weapon-free zone in Northern Europe.

In a statement of 6 June 1983, the Soviet Union expressed its readiness to respect the status of such a zone, and also to consider the question of certain measures relating to its own territory adjacent to the zone, which would promote the strengthening of its nuclear-weapon-free status. While France has expressed a cautious attitude with regard to the proposal, due to the geo-strategic importance of the Baltic region, the other nuclear-weapon States have not specifically addressed the subject, but their generally held views on nuclear-weapon-free zones would apply equally to this region.

G. SOUTH ASIA

The Assembly first considered the question of a denuclearized zone in South Asia in 1974, at the request of Pakistan, which saw an urgent need for such a zone.

In the debate, Pakistan noted that all the States of the region had already expressed opposition to the acquisition or introduction of nuclear weapons. In particular, it pointed out that India, both before and after the 1974 explosion of its nuclear device, had indicated that it would not develop or acquire nuclear weapons.

India made clear its support for the principle of establishing nuclear-weapon-free zones, provided that suitable conditions existed in a particular region and that the proposal was initiated and agreed to by the countries of the region. India believed, however, that South Asia could not be treated in isolation, as it was only a subregion, an integral part of the region of Asia and the Pacific. The existence of nuclear weapons in the region and the presence of foreign military bases in the Indian Ocean complicated the whole security environment and made the situation inappropriate for the establishment of a nuclear-weapon-free zone there, according to India.

Two separate resolutions submitted by India and Pakistan, closely reflecting their different positions, were both approved by the General Assembly on 9 December 1974. By the resolution initiated by India, the Assembly decided to give due consideration to any proposal for the creation of a nuclear-weapon-free zone in an appropriate region of Asia, after it had been developed and matured by the countries of the region. By the resolution initiated by Pakistan, the General Assembly urged the States of South Asia to begin consultations for the purpose of establishing such a zone and, in the interim, to refrain from any actions contrary to the achievement of that objective.

Between 1975 and 1984, 11 resolutions have been adopted by large majorities on the question, two in 1975 and one each year since 1976, initiated by Pakistan alone.

During the debates in the General Assembly, since 1974, Pakistan has consistently maintained that the generally recognized conditions for the establishment of a nuclear-weapon-free zone exist in South Asia. All the States of the region have already declared their opposition to the acquisition of nuclear weapons or to their introduction into the region. The five States possessing nuclear weapons have, in principle, indicated their support for or acceptance of the concept of establishing nuclear-weapon-free zones.

India's viewpoint is that the nuclear-weapon-free zone idea has become unrealistic and that the movement and deployment of nuclear weapons in various regions of the world by the nuclear-weapon States are fundamentally irreconcilable with the very idea of nuclear-weapon-free zones. At the second special session of the General Assembly on disarmament, in 1982, India's Foreign Minister stated that his country could not subscribe to the legitimization of the possession of nuclear weapons by a few Powers by agreeing to live under their professedly benign protection in the guise of a nuclear-weapon-free zone.

Zones of peace

The establishment of zones of peace is a relatively new concept developed in response to growing regional tensions and conflicts and increasing military presence of major Powers in various seas and oceans in the world. The 1978 Final Document of the special session on disarmament stated that the establishment of zones of peace in various regions of the world under appropriate conditions, to be clearly defined and determined freely by the States concerned in the zone, taking into account the characteristics of the zone and the principles of the Charter of the United Nations, and in conformity with international law, could contribute to strengthening the security of States within such zones and to international peace and security as a whole.

Indian Ocean

One such proposal on the agenda of the United Nations deals with the establishment of a zone of peace in the Indian Ocean, an idea first endorsed by the Heads of State or Government of Non-Aligned Countries, meeting at Lusaka in 1970.

In 1971 the General Assembly adopted a resolution by which it solemnly declared that the Indian Ocean, within limits to be determined, was designated for all time as a zone of peace. The Declaration called on the great Powers to enter into consultations with the littoral States with a view to halting the further expansion of their military presence in the Indian Ocean and eliminating from the area all their bases, military installations, nuclear weapons, and weapons of mass destruction and any manifestation of great-Power rivalry. It also called upon the littoral States, the permanent members of the Security Council and other major maritime users of the Indian Ocean to enter into consultations, with a view to implementing the Declaration of the Indian Ocean as a Zone of Peace.

The resolution was, however, adopted by a vote of 61 to none, with 55 abstentions, thus reflecting widely divergent views between Member States regarding practical aspects and implications of the Declaration.

In 1972, the General Assembly established a 15-member *Ad Hoc* Committee on the Indian Ocean (increased to 18 members in 1974, 23 in 1977, 45 in 1980 and 48 in 1984) to study the implications of the proposal. Since 1973, consideration of the issue in the General Assembly has generally centred on the report of the *Ad Hoc* Committee.

Following bilateral Soviet-American talks in 1977 to pursue possible limitations on military activities in the Indian Ocean, the United States and the Soviet Union stated in an agreed statement that there had been to date a certain measure of agreement on a number of questions, including the desirability of a staged approach, beginning with an agreement not to increase the current military presence, then moving on promptly to negotiations on reductions. The bilateral talks have not been resumed.

The question of the Indian Ocean as a zone of peace was given new attention at the 1978 special session of the General Assembly, but no progress was achieved on the outstanding issues concerning the implementation of the Declaration.

In 1979, a Meeting in New York of the Littoral and Hinterland States, which the members of the *Ad Hoc* Committee, the great Powers and the major maritime users of the Indian Ocean attended, recommended the holding of a Conference on the Indian Ocean, and proposed that the *Ad Hoc* Committee on the Indian Ocean undertake the preparatory work for it, including consideration of appropriate arrangements for any international agreement that might ultimately be reached.

The same year, the General Assembly decided to convene a Conference on the Indian Ocean in 1981 at Colombo, Sri Lanka, inviting the permanent members of the Security Council and major maritime users of the Indian Ocean to participate in it. The *Ad Hoc* Committee has not been able to make significant progress in the preparations for the Conference or to finalize dates for its convening. Although some progress on procedural matters, as well as substantive issues, has been made, the differences in approach between States remain wide, preventing the Committee from completing the preparatory work.

Zone of peace and co-operation of the South Atlantic
On the initiative of Brazil, the General Assembly included, in 1986, a "Zone of peace and co-operation of the South Atlantic" as a new item on its agenda. That same year, the General Assembly adopted a resolution, sponsored by a group of mainly African and Latin American States, by which it declared the South Atlantic to be a zone of peace and co-operation and called upon non-regional States, particularly the militarily significant ones, to respect the zone, especially through the reduction and eventual elimination of their military presence there. It also called for non-introduction of nuclear weapons, for

co-operation to eliminate all sources of tension in the zone, and for the Secretary-General to submit a report on the situation in 1987, on the basis of views of Member States. The resolution containing the Declaration was adopted with a vote of 124 in favour, 1 against and 8 abstentions. Among the nuclear powers, China, the United Kingdom and the Soviet Union voted in favour, the United States against, and France abstained.

In 1987, the Secretary-General's first report on the item contained views of 19 Member States. In its 1987 resolution, the General Assembly commended the efforts States were taking to promote peace and co-operation in the region, as reflected in that report, and urged them to continue their efforts and to refrain from any action inconsistent with the Charter or relevant resolutions, or which might aggravate tensions in the region. It also called on the United Nations system to assist in implementation of the concept and requested the Secretary-General to prepare a further report on the item for its 1988 regular session. The 1987 resolution was adopted by a vote of 122 to 1, with 8 abstentions, reflecting a similar pattern to that of 1986.

2

Can Nuclear-Free Zones be Enforceable?

The Chairman of the Atomic Energy Commission of Argentina alleged in July 1982 that the United Kingdom was in breach of the Treaty for the Prohibition of Nuclear Weapons in Latin America. This Treaty had been agreed in 1967, at Tlatelolco in Mexico, and was the first Treaty to establish a nuclear-free zone in a widely populated area. Previously, areas which had been declared to be free of nuclear weapons had included the Antarctic, Outer Space, and the Seabed. But Latin America was the first populated continent to forbid nuclear weapons anywhere in its region. A recent report by the United Nations summarises the provisions of this agreement:

> "The basic obligation of the parties to the Treaty, defined in article 1, is to use exclusively for peaceful purposes the nuclear material and facilities under their jurisdiction, and to prohibit and prevent in their respective territories the very presence of nuclear weapons for any purpose and under any circumstances.
> Parties to the Treaty also undertake to refrain from engaging in, encouraging or authorising, directly or indirectly, or in any way participating in the testing, use, manufacture, production, possession or control of any nuclear weapon".[1]

The Treaty of Tlatelolco has given rise to an Enforcement Committee, charged with the task of considering any violations or alleged violations.

> "OPANAL was set up in June 1969. Its control system includes safeguards to be negotiated with IAEA with respect to all the nuclear activities of the parties".[2]

When Argentina appeared before this Committee, it was seconded by Panama.

The status of Argentina in relation to the Treaty is itself a little ambiguous. The Argentines had signed the Treaty in 1967, but they had not actually ratified it subsequently, which would have been necessary if it were to be fully applied. However, the Treaty covers to whole area of Latin America, together with extensive areas in the surrounding oceans. Article 4 defines its scope:

"Article 4. *Zone of application*
1. The zone of application of this Treaty is the whole of the territories for which the Treaty is in force.
2. Upon fulfilment of the requirements of article 28, paragraph 1, the zone of application of this Treaty shall also be that which is situated in the western hemisphere within the following limits (except the continental part of the territory of the United States of America and its territorial waters): starting at a point located at 35° north latitude. 75° west longitude: from this point directly southward to a point at 30° north latitude. 75° west longitude: from there, directly eastward to a point at 30° north latitude. 50° west longitude: from there, along a loxodromic line to a point at 5° north latitude. 20° west longitude: from there, directly southward to a point at 60° south latitude. 20° west longitude: from there, directly westward to a point at 60° south latitude. 115° west longitude: from there, directly northward to a point at 0 latitude. 115° west longitude: from there, along a loxodromic line to a point at 35° north latitude. 150° west longitude: from there, directly eastward to a point at 35° north latitude. 75° west longitude".[3]

Britain had long previously endorsed the Treaty, by signing, in December 1967, the two protocols which were open to nuclear powers outside the region. These were "deposited" with the Government of Mexico two years later, thus activating all the procedures of the Treaty. One of the protocols involved states holding colonial territories in the area, and the other, nuclear states. They were devised in order to permit both colonial and nuclear powers to underwrite the non-nuclear status of the whole continent. But the British Government filed declarations reserving its position on certain matters within the province of the Treaty, which placed limits on its compliance.

> "When signing and ratifying Additional Protocol I and Additional Protocol II, the United Kingdom made the following declarations of understanding:
>
> In connection with Article 3 of the Treaty, defining the term 'territory' as including the territorial sea, airspace and any other space over which the state exercises sovereignty in accordance with 'its own legislation', the UK does not regard its signing or ratification of the Additional Protocols as implying recognition of any legislation which does not, in its view, comply with the relevant rules of international law.
>
> The Treaty does not permit the parties to carry out explosions of nuclear devices for peaceful purposes unless and until advances in technology have made possible the development of devices for such explosions which are not capable of being used for weapon purposes.
>
> The signing and ratification by the UK could not be regarded as affecting in any way the legal status of any territory for the international relations of which the UK is responsible, lying within the limits of the geographical zone established by the Treaty.
>
> Should a party to the Treaty carry out any act of aggression with the support of a nuclear weapon state, the UK would be free to reconsider the extent to which it could be regarded as committed by the provisions of Additional Protocol II.
>
> In addition, the UK declared that its undertaking under Article 3 of Additional Protocol II not to use or threaten to use nuclear weapons against the parties to the Treaty extends also to territories in respect of which the undertaking under Article 1 of Additional Protocol 1 becomes effective".[4]

The Argentine complaint of 1982 concerned the despatch of nuclear-powered submarines to the Falkland waters. It was, of course, a nuclear-powered submarine, the *Conqueror*, which sank the Argentine cruiser Belgrano, an event which marked off the irreversible deterioration of this conflict into all-out war. It is a nice question whether the arrival of nuclear submarines in South American waters was in fact a breach of the Treaty. As we have seen, Article One insists that nuclear material and installations in the region are solely employed for peaceful purposes. It is arguable that a nuclear submarine engaged in military action is not employing nuclear energy peacefully, even if it is not actually carrying nuclear explosives. Nonetheless, a "nuclear-weapon" in the meaning of the Treaty, is a device which can release nuclear energy "in an uncontrolled manner". Article Five lays down this criterion. It explicitly exempts propulsion mechanisms from the definition of "weaponry". No doubt because the Treaty is so specific, the Enforcement organisation did not feel able to take effective action on the original complaint. However, the Committee might have felt differently, had it been able to verify a report which appeared in the *New Statesman* two years later. This claimed to have hard evidence that a Polaris submarine had been sent to the South Atlantic.

> "One well-placed political source has already revealed to Tam Dalyell that a Polaris submarine was sent to the South Atlantic. Dalyell was informed that the submarine went as far south as Ascension; the likely target for a threatened or demonstration nuclear attack was said to be Cordoba, northern Argentina. The nuclear threat might have been used if any of the task force's capital ships — one of the carriers, or the troop ship *Canberra* — had been destroyed in a missile attack. The Polaris deployment was said to have been ordered in the wake of the sinking of HMS *Sheffield*, after ministers had to confront the possibility that Argentine air superiority and Exocet missiles could mean the military defeat of the British task force, and the rapid political extinction of the Thatcher government.
>
> The *New Statesman* has been able to confirm that a Polaris submarine was indeed deployed to this position. Details of the deployment are given in a series of highly classified telegrams sent to the British Embassy in Washington".[5]

Polaris, of course, is armed with what are undeniably nuclear weapons. If the *New Statesman* were able to authenticate their claim, then their evidence should certainly have been of interest to OPANAL, because, however distant Polaris remained from the Falkland zone, once it was redeployed in connection with the British task force, its weapons must have been trained against targets in the Treaty area.

Such claims may be difficult to substantiate. But they are not the only issues which should be considered by Tlatelolco's enforcement committee. Other ships than submarines steamed South during the Falklands/Malvinas war. It remains a crucial question to determine how many of these were nuclear armed. One important witness was Lieut. David Tinker, who died during the conflict. His moving letters to his family were published in 1982, and this is what they said:

> "One of our jobs out here is to transfer stores around between ships and yesterday I walked into the hangar and found a nuclear bomb there. I suppose if the USA and USSR have got 7,000 each, the chance of walking into one must be increased, but nevertheless I was rather surprised, and wondered if it was worth sheltering in the hangar any more. Of course, it turned out to be a drill round, full of concrete, that *Fort Austin*, now eventually going home, was taking back to England. I don't really know why we brought any down here. Loosing one off really would evaporate support for us by the EEC and Third World. Anyway, at least this lump of concrete is going back." [6]

Tinker is not at all alone in offering this testimony. It is apparently standard practice to issue such drill rounds to ships which may be called upon to deploy real ones. But how widely distributed were real sea-born nuclear armaments, particularly depth charges, and were any of them sent southwards? There were various press reports that British ships routinely deploy nuclear depth charges while they are on patrol. *The Times*, on 3rd November 1982, made a categorical statement that some of these were taken South.

> **"Frigates had nuclear weapons**
> Some British ships in the South Atlantic during the Falklands

campaign were carrying nuclear anti-submarine weapons (our Defence Correspondent writes).

Whitehall sources said that some of the frigates which went to the Falklands had been involved in exercises in the Mediterranean, and would have been routinely carrying anti-submarine nuclear bombs. Because they were diverted directly to the South Atlantic there would have been no opportunity to offload the weapons.

There would certainly have been no intention to use them in the South Atlantic, and ships which sailed from Britain would not have taken any nuclear weapons with them.

These bombs or depth charges are designed to be dropped from helicopters against deep lying submarines, and they explode beneath the sea's surface.

The fact that anti-submarine vessels carry nuclear depth charges has been an open secret for some time.

It was being said yesterday that until the weapons were "armed" they were safe, and that the arming or fusing mechanisms were stored in separate parts of the ships from the bombs themselves.

It is likely that the Prime Minister will be closely questioned on this issue. Mrs Margaret Thatcher will also be questioned about the fact that the 16,000-ton supply ship, *Fort Austin*, was diverted to the South Atlantic, sailing from Gibraltar on March 29".

Other sources have assumed that the redirection of British naval forces towards the South left them with no opportunity to divest themselves of nuclear depth charges before they went off to fight the Argentinians.

HMS *Sheffield*, which was sunk, took down, it was claimed, an entire cargo of such nuclear depth charges. A preliminary account of this appeared in the Latin America Weekly Report, on 12th November 1982:

"Another diplomatic storm is blowing up from the South Atlantic following claims that the British task force was carrying nuclear weapons during the Falklands/Malvinas conflict, in violation of the Tlatelolco treaty. The British government is refusing to respond to these accusations, claiming that any disclosures about its deployment of nuclear arms would run counter to national security interest.

According to defence experts in London, many of the British frigates and destroyers diverted to the area at the beginning of April would have been carrying tactical nuclear weapons designed for anti-submarine warfare. Nuclear depth charges are routinely carried by British warships on operations patrol in such areas as the North Atlantic, they say, and a large part of the fleet had no opportunity to offload any lethal weaponry before sailing for the South Atlantic.

A former naval secretary in the Thatcher government, Keith Speed, has cast doubt on the theory that the task force would have discharged its nuclear weapons at Ascension Island. Interviewed by BBC television this week, he said that he would have been surprised had the British force not carried nuclear arms to the Falklands.

Other defence sources say that the first effort was made to take the weapons out of the area after the sinking of the *General Belgrano* and the beginning of the 'shooting war'. This task was undertaken by an auxiliary support vessel, the *Fort Austin* which was close to HMS *Sheffield* when the destroyer was crippled by an Exocet missile.

It has been claimed that the *Sheffield* still had nuclear depth charges on board when it was hit, and that the British force spent the next three days attempting to remove them. The ship went down with a number still on board. These had to be recovered by naval divers.

The *Fort Austin*, meanwhile, is at the centre of another mystery surrounding the conflict. It has been established that the supply vessel sailed for the South Atlantic on 28 March, several days before the British Prime Minister claims she had any knowledge of the impending Argentine invasion of the islands".

Further allegations of the same kind have been made by Tam Dalyell:

". . . on March 29, ships and RFA vessels on Exercise Springtrain were ordered south . . . a number of those vessels carried nuclear weapons.

. . . some of the ships left Portsmouth in early April carrying nuclear weapons. . . . there was a row of gargantuan proportions about this in parts of Whitehall, as a result of which some, though not all, of the nuclear weapons were offloaded from the ships when they were at sea, before they got to the western approaches. . . . the Stenor Inspector and the Stenor Seasearch have been trying to retrieve nuclear devices from the tombs of HMS *Sheffield* and HMS *Coventry*.

. . . there is also the problem of lost nuclear depth charges from two lost Sea King mark 4 and two lost Sea King mark 5 helicopters . . . the hon. Member for Ashford (Mr Speed), the former Navy Minister, who lost his post, opined on *News Night* that he would be most surprised if the fleet were not carrying nuclear weapons".[7]

This account was also supported by an extensive account in the *New Statesman* which said:

> "The Navy has its own, relatively small stock of nuclear depth bombs. For some time after the Falklands War, they were not allowed to take them to sea. Ministers had belatedly discovered that the admirals had sent three quarters of the total British naval nuclear stockpile towards the South Atlantic battle zone.
>
> In peacetime, nuclear depth bombs are only allowed on board attack carriers (like HMS *Hermes* and HMS *Invincible*) and certain anti-submarine frigates. As all of the available ships in these classes set off for the Falklands in 1982, the 'War Cabinet' - the Oversea and Defence committee (South Atlantic) - were warned that most of the Navy's nuclear weapons would soon cross the equator".[8]

This was not the only claim in the *Statesman* piece, to which we shall return shortly.

At this point in the argument, what can be said about the case of the *Sheffield*? The HMS *Sheffield* was hit by an Exocet missile on May 4th. "She caught fire, and the crew abandoned ship", reported *The Times* next morning.

> "A massive pall of smoke appeared on the horizon as Sea King helicopters ferried casualties back to the flagship carrier HMS *Hermes*. The *Sheffield*, about 15 miles away, was completely blotted out by the smoke which formed a solid column from the sea to the clouds.
>
> As fire raged in the *Sheffield* a call was put out for hoses and pumping equipment to be dropped by helicopter. A frigate went alongside to help tackle the fires but three hours later it was decided to give the order to abandon ship because of the danger of a possible explosion of the *Sheffield*'s own Sea Dart missiles... The *Sheffield* was still drifting and on fire last night. She is thought to be the first British warship to be lost in battle since the Second World War (Henry Stanhope writes)".

In fact, at the time *Sheffield* sank, she was not "drifting" but under tow, as Mr Frank Allaun elicited from Mr Blaker in a parliamentary question on 23rd July 1982:

> "Mr Frank Allaun asked the Secretary of State for Defence how HMS *Sheffield* was sunk; and if he will make a statement.

Mr Blaker: HMS *Sheffield* sank under tow in heavy weather because sea water entered the hole in her side caused by the Argentine missile which struck her. To clarify any possible misunderstanding, I can state that there has never been any incident involving a British nuclear weapon leading to its loss or to the dispersal of radioactive contamination".

Was Mr Blaker admitting that the ship carried nuclear weapons which were not "lost" during the dying agony while the wreck was under tow? And why was the ship under tow *after* the order had been given to "abandon ship" for fear of exploding missiles? What, furthermore, of Mr Dalyell's charge that some of the weapons which sank with their ship were nuclear ones, for which the Stenor ships were later chartered to fish? These were the subject of another parliamentary question from Mr Frank Allaun, on 18th October 1982.

"Mr Frank Allaun asked the Secretary of State for Defence why two oil-fired underwater recovery vessels have been chartered to deal with HMS *Sheffield*.
Mr Blaker: No underwater recovery vessels have been chartered to deal with HMS *Sheffield*.
Mr Frank Allaun asked the Secretary of State for Defence, further to his reply to the hon. Member for Salford, East on 23 July, Official Report, c.340, if HMS *Sheffield* carried nuclear weapons.
Mr Blaker: It would not be in the interests of national security to depart from the long-standing practice, observed by successive Governments, neither to confirm nor deny the presence or absence of nuclear weapons in particular locations at given times".

Here we may see one of the great principles of Government equivocation at work: never lie if you can help it, but don't hasten to tell the truth. The Stenor ships were not "underwater recovery vessels", although at least one of them, the *Seaspread*, did carry a diving bell, as we were to learn on 1st September 1983 when Petty Officer Michael Harrison received the Queen's Gallantry Medal, as *The Times* told us, for "possibly the most dangerous task ever undertaken by a Royal Navy diving team".

Can Nuclear-Free Zones be Enforceable? 71

> "The medal was won while divers were recovering classified documents and equipment from ships sunk during the Falklands campaign last year. The nature of the material recovered has not been specified but it is thought to have included top secret code books and cryptographic equipment.
>
> The citation says that 'though working in extremely unpleasant, hazardous and dark conditions, and despite becoming entangled on two separate occasions with hanging debris, Harrison persevered with the task, putting himself at grave personal risk'.
>
> The action was in depths of more than 300 feet, and was carried out by a team of 27 naval divers.
>
> The operation was conducted from a chartered vessel, the 7,000 ton Stena *Seaspread*. It involved using a diving bell to carry the divers down.
>
> The divers left the diving bell but remained connected to it, while searching for the documents and equipment in the sunken ships.
>
> It is believed that much of the activity centred on *Coventry* which sank north of the Falklands.
>
> The recovery of the material has been regarded as a sensitive matter by the Royal Navy, not only because it was highly classified, but also because ships lost off the Falklands have been designated war graves".

Subsequently some doubt has been expressed about the role of the Stenor ships. Basing himself, no doubt, on this report, Duncan Campbell claimed in the *New Statesman* report to which we have already referred that they were in fact sent to retrieve cryptographic equipment and code books, not nuclear weapons.

> "There were thus no tactical nuclear weapons on board the surface ships sent south to the Falklands. The deep-diving vessel sent to recover 'equipment' from the sunken wreck of HMS *Coventry* -widely suspected at the time to have been an attempt to recover lost nuclear weapons - was in fact attempting to retrieve top secret cryptographic equipment and codebooks which the destroyer's captain had not had time to destroy. Type 42 destroyers, like *Coventry*, do not carry nuclear weapons in peacetime".[9]

Perhaps this may be true of the diving recovery work on the wreck of the *Coventry*: but are we expected to believe this of the *Sheffield*, which was under tow when it went down?

If they were not incinerated, why could the code books and machines not have been retrieved during these operations?

As Mr Dalyell asked at the time, it would be interesting to establish

> "whether our security services let our American allies know in advance that we British were taking nuclear weapons into their hemisphere against protocol 1 of the Treaty of Tlatelolco of which both Britain and the Americans are signatories. The related question is, what do we now say as British people to the non-aligned nations which, meeting in Delhi, asked us to remove nuclear weapons from land and sea areas around the Falklands? It is all very well to say that we would never have used nuclear weapons. That seems to be the received wisdom. However, can we be quite sure? Let us suppose, heaven help us, that *Invincible, Hermes* or *Canberra*, hit by a torpedo which actually exploded, had gone down with a loss of life comparable to the sinking of the *Belgrano*. There might have been an irresistible demand, in a losing situation, to go ahead - as was, indeed, discussed in certain quarters - to bomb granaries and airports in Argentina. Those who have nuclear weapons in desperate situations may be tempted not to be too choosy about how they use them. The whole operation was a hideous gamble, with no long-term prize for this country".[10]

On June 3rd 1983, I wrote to the Secretary-General of the United Nations on some of these questions:[11]

> Mr Javier Perez de Cuellar, Secretary-General, United Nations, New York, USA
> Dear Secretary General,
> For some time now British public opinion has been disturbed by questions about the conduct of the Falklands War, and in particular by a serious controversy about the sinking of the Argentinian cruiser *Belgrano*.
> The charges against Mrs Thatcher have been tersely summarised in an 'information sheet' (number 11) published by *Ecoropa* under the title *Falklands War: The Disturbing Truth*. There are two main counts in this indictment:
> 1. The cruiser *Belgrano* was sunk 'so as to make peace impossible' even while an agreement for Argentine withdrawal from the islands was reaching its final stages.
> 2. That nuclear weapons were taken to the South Atlantic.
> These matters are very grave and they surely merit a special enquiry in Britain. I shall certainly give all support to the demand

for this enquiry if I am elected to the House of Commons on June 9th.

But these matters do not only affect the people of the United Kingdom. Both raise profound international questions.

The first charge, of sabotaging peace talks by sinking the *Belgrano*, amounts to an accusation that Mrs Thatcher or her agents breached the Nuremburg Principles of 1946, which provide the most authoritative summary of the decisions of the post-war War Crimes Tribunal. This Tribunal received unanimous endorsement for its findings at the General Assembly of the United Nations (see Resolution 95-i). The precise infraction alleged against Mrs Thatcher or her agents is covered in Principle VI as a 'crime against peace', qualified in Article a(i) as 'planning, preparation, initiation or waging a war... in violation of international ... agreements or assurances'. It will be remembered that UN Resolution 502 demanded 'immediate cessation of hostilities' and withdrawal of Argentine forces, and called for a 'diplomatic solution' respecting the UN Charter.

The second charge of sending nuclear weapons into the war zone, alleges a direct breach of the terms of the Treaty of Tlatelolco, under which Britain recognises the status of Latin America as a nuclear-free zone.

Can you advise us about how these issues could be properly investigated? We are particularly concerned about the enforcement of the Treaty of Tlatelolco, since we have been active in encouraging the proposal to create a nuclear-free zone in Europe. Clearly, the possible breach of the Latin American nuclear-free zone raises major questions. Disregard of nuclear-free zone arrangements would, if it were to go unopposed, totally negate the intentions of the UN Special Session on Disarmament, which commended such zones as an important confidence building measure.

At the same time, the legal implications of the sinking of the *Belgrano* are also deeply serious. There would be no 'crime against peace' if there had been no UN Resolution 502, and if diplomatic approaches had been spurned on all or either sides. The armed forces on both sides were in no position to know about the extent of diplomatic progress. It is unlikely that the diplomats could expect to have detailed knowledge about military dispositions. Only at the point where decisions could be taken, weighing together both diplomatic and military issues, is there any possibility of a 'crime against peace'. For this reason, it seems to me that the United Nations is the only relevant body to investigate this issue.

With great respect,
Yours sincerely,
Ken Coates

On 26th August 1983, I received a reply from Mr Richard Wathen:

> Dear Mr Coates,
> I should like to refer to your letter of 3 June 1983, addressed to the Secretary General concerning matters pertaining to the conduct of the Falklands War.
>
> We have carefully analysed the two issues you have raised in your letter which are of undoubted importance. The alleged introduction of nuclear weapons into the South Atlantic Zone has been the object of a resolution by the General Conference of the Organisation for the Prohibition of Nuclear Weapons in Latin America (we are attaching a copy in Spanish, the only language available at this time). This Organisation might in fact be competent also to initiate an investigation on this matter.
>
> As far as the United Nations is concerned, any investigation would have to follow the adoption of a resolution by one of the two political organs of the Organisation already seized of the question of the Falklands (Malvinas), namely the General Assembly or the Security Council. Such resolution would have to be sponsored by one or more member states.
> Yours sincerely,
> Richard W. Wathen, *Principal Officer*,
> Department of Political Affairs,
> Trusteeship and Decolonisation.

ORGANISATION FOR THE PROHIBITION OF NUCLEAR ARMS
IN LATIN AMERICA

GENERAL CONFERENCE
Eighth (Ordinary) Period of Sessions
Item 18 on the Agenda
KINGSTON, JAMAICA: 16-19 May 1983

CG/RES.170 (VIII) 18 May 1983

Resolution 170(VIII) - Reports of the introduction of nuclear arms by the United Kingdom of Great Britain and Northern Ireland in the zone and areas of the Islas Malvinas, Georgias Del Sur and Sandwich Del Sur.

The General Conference,
Considering that the governments signatory to the Treaty of Tlatelolco have categorically expressed their determination that nuclear energy be used in Latin America exclusively for peaceful purposes and, to this end, reaffirmed their sovereign decision to establish a military de-nuclearised zone in order to keep their

territories free, forever, of nuclear armaments:

Considering that the Argentinian Republic has denounced at various international gatherings the presence of nuclear weaponry aboard vessels of the British naval forces which operated in areas within the geographical zone designated by Paragraph 2 of Article 4 of the Treaty in connection with the conflict in the Islas Malvinas (Falkland Islands) and the South Georgias and South Sandwich Islands, pointing out in the light of this event the significance of countries in possession of nuclear weapons engaging in operations in which nuclear energy is put to non-peaceful uses:

Considering that spokesmen for the government of the United Kingdom have on several occasions declared that it would be inconvenient, for reasons of national security, to abandon the established practice, observed by successive governments, of neither confirming nor denying the presence or absence of nuclear weapons at a specific place and a given time;

Considering that the United Kingdom of Great Britain and Northern Ireland has made the declaration which appears in the document S/Inf. 261 of 11 May 1983;

Having regard to the fact that the Organisation for the Prohibition of Nuclear Arms in Latin America (OPANAL) has a duty to supervise compliance with the obligations laid down by the Treaty of Tlatelolco;

Reaffirming the need for a balance of responsibilities and obligations affecting states which possess nuclear arms and those which do not possess them;

Resolves:

1. *To note with concern* the complaint formulated by the Argentinian Republic concerning the introduction of nuclear arms, by the United Kingdom of Great Britain and Northern Ireland, into areas included in the geographical zone designated in Paragraph 2 of Article 4 of the Treaty of Tlatelolco.

2. *To take note* of the declaration by the United Kingdom of Great Britain and Northern Ireland to which the fourth Considering paragraph of this Resolution refers, and which states in its leading paragraphs: "The Government of the United Kingdom has scrupulously complied with its obligations under Additional Protocol I to the Treaty for the Prohibition of Nuclear Arms in Latin America and has not deployed nuclear weapons in areas for which, *de jure* or *de facto*, it is internationally responsible and which are located within the limits of the geographical zone established in the said Treaty. Moreover, the Government has scrupulously complied with its obligations under Additional Protocol II to the Treaty and has not deployed nuclear weapons in areas where the Treaty is in force".

3. *To take note* of the important presentations and declarations formulated by the Delegations of Argentina and the United

Kingdom at this General Conference.

4. *To express its concern* at the fact that in areas within the geographical zone designated by Paragraph 2 of Article 4 of the Treaty, submarines powered by nuclear energy should have been employed in warlike actions.

5. *To exhort*
all States in respect of which the Treaty and its Additional Protocols are not in force, to take the necessary steps in accordance with Article 28 to complete the process of military de-nuclearisation in the relevant zone defined by Paragraph 2 of Article 4 of the Treaty itself.

6. *To reaffirm* the commitment of all States linked by the Treaty of Tlatelolco and its Additional Protocols, to refrain from carrying out all actions which might endanger the status of military denuclearisation of Latin America and to recommend that the Council of the Organisation closely supervise its strict enforcement.

7. *To communicate* to the General Assembly of the United Nations in its 38th Period of Sessions, and to the Disarmament Committee, the text of the present Resolution, together with the declarations made on the subject in the course of this Conference.

(Approved in the Forty-ninth Session, held on 19 May 1983).
Translated from the Spanish by Mike Mullan.

In order to understand the significance of the British Government's statement summarised in the second point of this Resolution, we need to remind ourselves of the two distinct commitments which arise, not only under Protocol I, to which Tam Dalyell referred in his complaint, but also under Protocol II of the Treaty. Protocol I implies the exclusion of nuclear weapons from the narrow area of the territorial waters of the Islands themselves. But Protocol II, strictly interpreted, enjoins their exclusion from the very much wider area established in Article 4 of the Treaty, to which we have made reference. This, it will be seen, covers hundreds of kilometres of the South Atlantic over a zone extending far to the East and North of the Islands themselves. The question of whether the Treaty was or was not "in force" could be argued to turn on the significance of the fact that Argentina has signed but not ratified the Treaty. We may conclude that this less than frank manipulation between protocols was going on, by referring to the results of a parliamentary question in the House of Lords on 21st December 1982:

> "Lord Jenkins of Putney asked Her Majesty's Government: Whether they have at any time been in breach of their obligations under the Treaty for the Prohibition of Nuclear Weapons in Latin America.
>
> Lord Belstead: I can assure the noble Lord that the Government have at all times complied, and continue to comply, with their obligation not to introduce nuclear weapons into the territory or territorial waters for which it is internationally responsible within the Treaty's zone of application".

If, as may be surmised, the British Government is seeking, by use of this formulation, praying its respect of the three-mile limit then applying to the Islands, to cover for nuclear intrusions into the broad area of the Treaty's waters, then it surely constitutes a breach of the aims of the Treaty. Is it not the external protocol, giving the guarantee that nuclear powers will respect the zone, which is the very heart of the Treaty?

For all who are concerned with the development of nuclear-free zones as an alternative to the proliferation of nuclear weapons worldwide, this question has considerable urgency. The enforcement of the Treaty of Tlatelolco is a duty, not only for Latin Americans, but also, and perhaps above all, for the citizens of the nuclear powers. If this Treaty is to be disregarded, then the consequences are deeply serious: to allow a central part of the United Nations' strategy for nuclear disarmament to be rubbished, is to negate the hope for legal and democratic regulation of international disputes.

It is for this reason that further enquiries are urgently necessary.

Footnotes

1. United Nations Department for Disarmament Affairs: *The United Nations and Disarmament: 1945-1985*, UN, New York, 1985, p.93.

2. *Ibid.*

3. United Nations Department for Disarmament Affairs: Status of Multilateral Arms Regulation and Disarmament Agreements, Second Edition, 1982, UN, New York, 1983, pp.48-49.

4. Stockholm International Peace Research Institute: *Arms Control: A Survey and Appraisal of Multilateral Agreements*, Taylor and Francis, 1978, pp.190-191.

5. Duncan Campbell and John Rentoul, "Falklands: All Out War", *New Statesman*, 24th August 1984, p.9.

6. David Tinker: *A Message from the Falklands*, Penguin, 1982, p.208.

7. Tam Dalyell, MP: *Thatcher's Torpedo*, Cecil Woolf, 1983, pp.32-33.

8. Duncan Campbell: "Too Few Bombs to go Round", *New Statesman*, 29th November 1985.

9. *New Statesman*, 29th November 1985, ibid.

10. Tam Dalyell, *ibid*, p.33.

11. Ken Coates: *The Most Dangerous Decade*, Spokesman, 1984, pp.73-77.

3

Israel's Bomb: The First Victim

On the 6th July 1987, thirty-six British Members of Parliament wrote to the Norwegian Nobel Committee to nominate Mr. Mordechai Vanunu of Israel for the Nobel Peace Prize. Since Mr. Vanunu was currently held in prison in Jerusalem, this was an unusual nomination. What were the reasons for it?

"On the 5th October 1986" reports the proposal, "Mr. Vanunu published in the *Sunday Times* a detailed story about the Israeli Government's nuclear bomb factory near Dimona in Southern Israel. In addition to a detailed description, Mr. Vanunu furnished the newspaper with photographs and diagrams, and his account of the plan was found to be "entirely authentic." by a number of international experts who subsequently examined it.

The threat of nuclear proliferation into various hot spots around the world is one of the major perils confronting the international community. It takes prodigious courage for a private citizen to confront his own Government on such a sensitive issue. Mr. Vanunu has paid a very heavy penalty. For revealing his knowledge, he was kidnapped in Rome, and secretly taken to Israel, where he has been locked in solitary confinement. Even his family have now been denied the right to visit him. Although he faces a death sentence, his trial is being conducted in secrecy."[1]

As the parliamentarians point out, there is reason for deep concern about the Israeli Government's preparation of nuclear weapons. The decision is a provocation: if it were not challenged, on what basis could any impartial person reproach the Arab States if they were to follow suit? The nuclearization of conflict or potential conflict in one of the world's hottest of "hot spots" can only be a terribly dangerous precedent.

But we should observe from the very outset of this discussion that Mr. Vanunu's kidnap is itself an illegal act, which has no conceivable justification in international conventions. We cannot doubt that the Italian Government would have refused to extradite Mr. Vanunu for trial, on any of the evidence which is available. Vanunu's revelations serve to defend the non-proliferation regime throughout the world, and are clearly a matter of conscience. Such disclosures have aroused disquiet in Italy and England, and any judge in either country would find them quite ineligible for criminal reprisals.

There can be no doubt that Vanunu is a courageous and deeply conscientious person, who has suffered from the most outrageous treatment by the Israeli authorities. We shall return to this question.

First, however, we must concern ourselves with the substantive issues in this case. What caused the paranoid responses of the Israeli State in this matter? After all, it is not common for states to range across the territories of friendly countries, in order to bring about the abduction of political dissidents. Vanunu was spirited from London to Rome, where he was forcibly drugged, and chained up for transportation to Tel Aviv. There does not appear to be any doubt that his departure from Italy was procured by illegal means, in violation of Italian laws and exit formalities. Such extreme measures put the normal conduct of inter-governmental relations under severe challenge. However we examine this affair, there can be no doubt of the culpability of the Israeli authorities. In order to understand this sequence of events, it is necessary to refer back to a succession of Israeli policy statements on the issue which is really at stake: that of nuclear proliferation.

There is, of course, a long history of public statements by various Israeli spokesmen, on all the issues of nuclear non-proliferation policy. But for the purposes of this argument we have no need to retrace our steps further than the 7th June 1981, when the Osirak nuclear reactor was bombed by Israeli aeroplanes. In a statement purporting to justify this action, the Government of Israel pledged its continuing support for the principle of non-proliferation, for multilateral arms control agreements, and for UN decisions against nuclear proliferation. The statement, *"The Iraqi Threat - Why Israel had to Act"*, rehearsed a catalogue of diplomatic initiatives by Israel, in this sense:

"Israel ratified the partial Test Ban Treaty on 15th January 1964, and the Outer Space Treaty on 18th February 1977. On 10th June 1968, Israel voted in favour of United Nations Resolution 2373 adopting the text of the NPT. It did so in the belief that this would enhance practical and satisfactory solutions for the prevention of nuclear weapons proliferation. In subsequent years, Israel has studied the NPT's various aspects in reference to the conditions prevailing in the Middle East, and has concluded that the turbulent and constantly shifting conditions still prevailing in the region prevent the Treaty's implementation in good faith on the part of many of the States in it.

A central assumption of the NPT is the existence of conditions of peace which do not exist today in the area. With the exception of Egypt, the Arab States do not recognize Israel's right to exist, are continuously preparing themselves to destroy it, and are mostly opposed to negotiating with it. A number of Arab States have added reservations with regard to Israel to their signature of disarmament treaties or of the NPT. In addition, Israel is aware that more than a dozen Arab States, as well as Pakistan, are not party to the NPT, and that a number of Arab signatories to the NPT have not fulfilled their obligations in accordance with it."

After listing a series of allegations concerning the development of nuclear facilities in different Arab countries, the Israeli statement continued:

"Israel believes that the most effective way to prevent the spread of nuclear weapons to the Middle East is the creation of a nuclear weapon-free zone in the region, modelled on the Tlatelolco Treaty, which is based on the initiative of the States of the region, and direct negotiations among them. Israel has repeatedly given expression to this idea and, since 1974, had advocated it *annually* (my emphasis, KC) at the United Nations General Assembly."[2]

This statement was enlarged in the declaration of the then Foreign Minister Shamir to the United Nations General Assembly on the 1st October 1981. After accusing Iraq of assembling "all the ingredients required for the development of nuclear weapons", he went on:

"Israel had to conclude that a country which acquired a complete fuel cycle and is openly bent on the destruction of Israel will not balk at going ahead with its programme, whether or not it is party to the NPT.

Let me take this opportunity to reiterate Israel's policy that *it will not be the first country in the Middle East to introduce nuclear weapons into the region*. (my emphasis, KC) Faced as it is with the stark realities of the Middle East, Israel must insist on distinguishing between spurious and genuine safety. The only genuine way to remove the nuclear

Israel's Bomb: The First Victim

threat to the Middle East can be found in the establishment of a nuclear weapon-free zone, freely and directly negotiated among the countries of the region, and based on mutual assurances, on the pattern of the Tlatelolco Treaty of Latin America."[3]

Evidently, these statements look very sick in the light of Vanunu's comprehensive revelations about the Dimona nuclear research centre. One travels to Dimona along the road from Beersheba to Sodom. As the *Sunday Times* reported, a fleet of forty buses make this journey every day, and among those travelling on them are 150 workers who are employed in the Machon 2 building which straddles six subterranean levels in which "the components of nuclear weapons are produced and machined into warhead parts". Vanunu started work in Machon 2 in 1977. His revelations were shown by the *Sunday Times* to Dr. Theodor Taylor in the United States and after thirty-six hours of deliberations he said:

"There should no longer be any doubt that Israel is, *and for at least a decade, has been*, (my emphasis, KC) a fully-fledged nuclear weapons state. The Israeli nuclear weapons programme is considerably more advanced than indicated by any previous reports or conjectures of which I am aware. The information obtained from Vanunu's statements and photographs as presented to me are entirely consistent with a present Israeli capacity to produce at least five to ten nuclear weapons a year that are significantly smaller, lighter, and more efficient than the first types of nuclear weapons developed by the US, USSR, UK, France and China."

Both Dr. Taylor and Professor Frank Barnaby, the British specialist, were deeply shocked by photographs of a component machined in lithium deuteride. Both authorities believed that the devices shown in this and other photographs provided did not show "a simple atom bomb but a thermo-nuclear bomb". As the *Sunday Times* itself concluded: "The verdict of ten senior and expert scientists approached by the *Sunday Times* is that Vanunu's testimony cannot be faulted".[5]

If we accept this evidence, it is evident at once that Mr. Shamir's statement at the United Nations General Assembly must have been quite untrue, even at the time he made it. If Israel had already become "the first country in the Middle East to introduce nuclear weapons into the region", the promise to refrain from this action in future can only be understood as a deliberate and particularly damaging dishonesty. There are many ways to mislead the General Assembly without telling actual lies: but on the 1st October 1981 it is quite evident that Mr. Shamir went far beyond any licence which might conceivably be given to diplomatic evasion. His statement was absolute and categorical: he now owes the United Nations an explanation.

Perhaps the Israeli spokesman is not the only diplomat to have offended in this way, grave though it is to do so. There is, however, a more serious question. On this and a larger number of other occasions, as the Israeli Government statement points out, Israel has advocated the conclusion of a Treaty establishing a nuclear weapon-free zone throughout the Middle East. To assure the United Nations that Israel "will not be the first" to introduce nuclear weapons, and to demand the creation of a nuclear-free zone, whilst all the time producing and storing a full-scale nuclear arsenal, is to present a package calculated to undermine not only the United Nations but also the very idea of nuclear-free zones. That such misleading declarations have been uttered "annually" hardly mitigates the offence. The Israeli Government itself continuously insists that it wishes to see the establishment of adequate guarantees in this field. As it argues in the text we have already cited: "Restraints of a technical or institutional nature alone can hardly protect the area from nuclear proliferation." To appeal for the creation of a nuclear free-zone, whilst at the same time secretly building a major stockpile of nuclear weapons, is to furnish an unusually compelling kind of proof for this statement!

It remains true that of all the panoply of partial disarmament measures considered in the United Nations Special Session on Disarmament in 1978, one is preeminent. The agreement to create and enforce nuclear-free zones is among the more achievable objectives for States, and for their peoples, in many parts of the world. Not only in Latin America, but also in other zones such as the South Pacific, or the continent of Africa, the idea of constituting a nuclear-free zone has captured widespread popular support, and mobilized the support of many of the Governments in the areas concerned. In this connection, the experience of the campaign for European Nuclear Disarmament is that millions of Europeans have come to share the view that a nuclear-free zone in all Europe is both possible and desirable. Already there are intense practical negotiations in smaller sub-regions of the European continent, to begin to put in place some parts of what many hope will be a larger jigsaw, sanitising larger and larger areas. The particular merit of such proposals is that they provide a practical linkage between the activities of popular movements and the relevant governments, and they make a space in which a global public opinion can grow. Such an international public mobilisation is crucial to the maintenance of peace through a period of unprecedented crisis, both economic and political.

As the popular pressure has begun to develop, the United Nations system has taken on a more material reality for millions of people, so that the vast demonstration which accompanied the opening of the Second Special Session could convince many of the real existence of a new potential in the world.

But the Vanunu case poses a most dire challenge to all this positive thinking. The creation of the Israeli bomb, and its analogue in South Africa, confronts us with a quite new, and very major problem of enforcement of non-nuclear commitments in the military field.

The first lesson of the Vanunu story is clear: that considerable agnosticism is required when evaluating the successive claims of governments which are poised upon the acquisition of nuclear weapons. In retrospect, we now see the French involvement in Israeli nuclear programmes, and in the initial provision of the Dimona reactor in a very clear and sinister light. It is not at all surprising that Israeli leaders can mislead the United Nations, when we remember how they responded to the enquiries of the United States Government about what was going on at Dimona in the early 1960s. "We are building a textile factory", replied the Israelis. Now it is possible to see the meaning of various other key events in Israel's military evolution: the French embargo on arms supplies; the pressures of the American administration for ratification of the Non-Proliferation Treaty; the later hiatus over the supply of Pershing missiles. There has evidently been some serious complicity in this act of nuclear provocation, and there are embarrassing questions to be answered in more than one of the world's chancellories.

The first serious effort to find answers to these questions has been extensively reported in the

Christian Science Monitor [6]. The newspaper gives an account of a study by Gary Milhollin, which makes precise allegations of a violation of undertakings given to the Norwegian Government, when a quantity of heavy water was supplied in 1959.

Mordechai Vanunu has recorded that 88 pounds of plutonium are produced each year at Dimona, which quantity can be used to make something between eight and ten bombs annually. Heavy water is necessary to this process, and the Norwegian delivery amounted to 20 tons. It was obtained against firm pledges that it would only be used for peaceful purposes. It was agreed that the Norwegian authorities could maintain rights of control and inspection over the uses to which the water was put. But Milhollin has established that, up to the moment of Vanunu's revelations, no attempt was made from Oslo to monitor the observance of these pledges.

After the *Sunday Times* publication of the real situation at Dimona, the Norwegian Government requested Israel to allow an appropriate inspection of the uses of the heavy water. It proposed that the International Atomic Energy Agency (IAEA) should be invited to investigate and report. In September, the Israelis refused any such inspection. At the talks in question, the Israelis conceded that the heavy water was being used at Dimona, and that plutonium was being produced with it. Per Paust, the spokesman of the Norwegian Foreign Ministry, has been reported as saying that the Israelis maintain that any IAEA report would be biased, and continue to insist that they have breached none of their obligations to Norway.

It seems that the rights of the Norwegian authorities, under international law, are comprehensive. Whether or not it can be proved that the heavy water from Norway was abused for military work, the Norwegians are entitled to the inspection for which they have asked. If tests establish that plutonium has been produced, then the Norwegians have the right to see the product, and if the weapons have been manufactured they have the right to insist upon them being dismantled. Mr Paust also believes that the water could be recalled, although no-one is quite sure how much other heavy water, from other sources, may have been supplied to Israel. What is known is that the Americans have furnished Israel with 3.9 tons, and that additional supplies have come from France. "French" heavy water originates either from the USA or Norway, and is theoretically subject to the same controls agreed between Norway and Israel. Therefore the French had no right to re-export it to Israel without permission, and any "French" heavy water used for military purposes could be recalled, not only by the French Government, but also by the American or Norwegian Governments.

Milhollin's estimate is that Dimona uses 36 tons of heavy water. The American water has been under control since it was moved from Dimona, and the IAEA has inspected it. But it has not been tested to elucidate whether, while it was at Dimona, it was employed in Plutonium refinement. American experts did visit Dimona annually from 1963 to 1969, but they conducted none of the relevant tests, either.

If the Norwegian authorities persist in their enquiries, as they undoubtedly should, then it is evident that similar enquiries should be initiated by the French and American Governments. The IAEA should also be pressed to be more curious than it hitherto has been. All these questions are absolutely urgent, if the non-proliferation regime is to retain any credibility whatever.

But it is equally imperative to re-examine a whole history of nuclear co-operation between Israel and South Africa, with the same open-mindedness.

The nuclear test which took place in the South Atlantic on 22nd September 1979 was monitored by a United States satellite. The explosion, which gave off a characteristic double flash, took place at a height of eight kilometres, which is commensurate with the performance of the G5 Howitzer, which has been manufactured in South Africa since the United States supplied Pretoria with a range of modern artillery delivery systems. The Americans have also supplied the South Africans with 300,000 shell casings, adequate to deliver a two to three kiloton nuclear device.

It has been confirmed that forces of the South African fleet were present in the South Atlantic in the area of the explosion at the time that it took place. And further, it is credibly alleged that the 1979 explosion was a joint Israeli-South African achievement, as necessary to the Israelis for verifying their technology as it was to the South Africans for threatening their neighbours. That the United Nations were persuaded to record a verdict of "not proven" about this explosion tells us a good deal about the respect of some of its experts for the rules of evidence.[7]

However, new evidence continually appears, and it would be instructive to reopen this enquiry in order to evaluate it. Since we now know that the allegations of Fuad Jabber, or the judgements, from a different perspective, of Robert E. Harkavy,[8] were founded on realistic assumptions, it becomes necessary to evaluate the contemporary analyses of Israeli-South African co-operation, all over again.

Valuable evidence for such a new investigation has been presented by Jane Hunter in her most disturbing work on *Israeli Foreign Policy.*[9]

"In 1965, after South Africa brought its Safari safeguarded reactor on line, Israeli scientists began advising South Africa on their Safari 2 research reactor.[10] In 1968, Professor Ernst Bergmann, the "father" of Israel's nuclear program, went to South Africa and spoke strongly in favour of bilateral co-operation on the development of nuclear technology.[11]

According to the authors of a novelized treatment of Israel's nuclear program - barred from publication by the Israeli censor -as early as 1966, South Africa had invited Israel to use its land or ocean space for a nuclear weapons test. Led at that time by Prime Minister Levi Eshkol, Israel declined the invitation. However, according to the Israeli authors, whose sources included Shimon Peres, an enthusiastic intimate of the Israeli nuclear program, and Knesset Member Eliyah Speizer, during his April 1976 visit to Israel Premier Vorster again extended the invitation to Israel to conduct a nuclear test.

It is commonly held that Israel wanted a test venue far from the Middle East in order to uphold its longtime position that it would not be the first to introduce nuclear weapons into the region.[12] This "position", hinging on some arcane reading of the word "introduce", is as meaningless as the endlessly heard term "peace process".

The following year, a Soviet satellite picked up unmistakable signs of preparation for a nuclear test in the Kalahari Desert. Fearing that such a test "might trigger an ominous escalation of the nuclear arms race," the U.S., Britain, France and West Germany joined the USSR in pressuring South Africa to abort the test.[13] As to the bomb that was to be tested, "'I know some intelligence people who are convinced with damn near certainty that it was an Israeli nuclear device', said a high-ranking Washington official."[14]

At three o'clock in the morning on September 22, 1979, Israel and South Africa conducted a nuclear weapons test where the South Atlantic and Indian Oceans merge.[15]

A newly recalibrated U.S. Vela intelligence satellite[16] recorded the characteristic double flash of light. It was a small blast, designed to leave very little evidence.[17] The CIA told the National Security Council that a two- or three-kiloton bomb had been exploded in "a joint South African-Israeli test".[18] A Navy official revealed that U.S. spy planes over the test area had been waved away by South African Navy ships and forced to land secretly in Australia.[19] The CIA knew (and later told Congress) that South African ships were conducting secret manoeuvers at the exact site of the test.[20] The South African military attaché in Washington made the first ever request to the U.S. National Technical Information Service for a computer search on detection of nuclear explosions and orbits of the Vela satellite.[21]

Almost immediately the Carter Administration convened a special panel to conduct an investigation of the incident. The panel heard reports from the U.S. Naval Research Laboratory, the Defense Intelligence Agency, and the CIA; and representatives of the Los Alamos National Laboratory, the Department of Energy and the State Department presented evidence to the panel supporting the occurrence of a nuclear explosion. Their findings were summarily dismissed by the Carter White House, which after a delay of seven months declared:

"Although we cannot rule out the possibility that this (Vela) signal was of nuclear origin, the panel considers it more likely that the signal was one of the zoo events (reception of signals of unknown origin under anomalous circumstances), possibly a consequence of the impact of a small meteoroid on the satellite".[22]

Moreover, as new information became available, it was simply ignored. In one critical instance, evidence of radiation observed in the thyroid glands of Australian sheep was discounted. The initial lack of this "smoking gun," traces of radiation, suggested to a Los Alamos scientist that the low-yield weapon tested had been a neutron bomb. However, the Carter panel had used the absence of radiation as a prime excuse in its cover-up.[23]

Many who had been involved with the investigation were aghast and wondered why the Carter White House was "equivocating".[24] Some within the government said that the Carter Administration was hiding behind the "zoo" theory to avoid dealing with the political headaches that would accompany acknowledgement of the test. An affirmative report might have affected the ongoing negotiations over the creation of Zimbabwe in which South African co-operation was needed and upset the upcoming Democratic Party primary campaign against Sen. Edward Kennedy."[25]

But beyond that, as a State Department official explained, coming clean on the test "would be a major turning point in our relations with South Africa and Israel if we determined conclusively that either had tested a nuclear bomb. It makes me terribly nervous just to think about it."[26] Of course by deciding to ignore reality the Carter administration - and following in its footsteps, the Reagan Administration, which went on record May 21, 1985 as upholding the Carter "verdict"[27] - destroyed the already tattered credibility of the nonproliferation posture of the U.S. There was no challenge forthcoming from Congress. Quite the contrary: in 1981 Representatives Stephen Solarz and Jonathan Bingham withdrew legislation they had introduced calling for a cutoff of U.S. aid to nations manufacturing nuclear weapons after they learned from the State Department "that such a requirement might well trigger a finding by the Administration that Israel has manufactured a bomb."[28] The U.S. government turned its back on the potential victims of Israeli and South African nuclear aggression, and stuck its head in the sand like an ostrich.

Five years later, the Washington Office on Africa Educational Fund in cooperation with Congressman John Conyers (D-MI), the Congressional Black Caucus Foundation and the World Campaign Against Military and Nuclear Collaboration with South Africa issued a report on the 1979 nuclear weapons test. Based on documents obtained from the government under the Freedom of Information Act, the report detailed scientific evidence not taken into account by the Carter panel. It demonstrated conclusively that a cover-up had been perpetrated by the Carter Administration. Written by Howard University Professor Ronald Walters, the report warned that the cover-up, "coupled with the Reagan Administration's subsequent allowance of an increase in nuclear aid to South Africa has serious implications for international peace and security."[29]

The sponsors of the report urged that the investigation be reopened under the auspices of the National Academy of Sciences and the National Academy of Engineers, and also called for a Congressional investigation and "the release to the public of all pertinent information."[30]"

Of course, whether enquiries are reopened in the USA, or the United Nations, or not, many African States are deeply uneasy about these events. Unsurprisingly, the conclusions which they have drawn reflect considerable alarm. A number of black African countries have quite reasonably concluded that they are prospective candidates for nuclear bombardment by South Africa. No Government in the front-line states can possibly ignore this threat. Persistent cross-border military activity by the apartheid regime is a permanent fact of political life in the southern part of the African continent.

But it is not only in the front-line states that alarm bells have been ringing. As Oye Ogunbadejo informs us:

"Nigeria, for example, sees itself as ... a potential target. Lagos has consistently argued that any improvements in South Africa's military power and nuclear capability, with the assistance of the West, pose direct military threats to Nigeria, and make it an open target of long-range nuclear attack. Alhaji Shehu Shagari, as President, continued to emphasize the need for his country to catch up with South Africa in the nuclear field. For the time being, however, Nigeria's efforts are geared, essentially, towards energy purposes."[31]

Yet, Ogunbadejo cites other prominent African spokesmen who are very impatient with the restriction of nuclear capacity to the civilian sector. Thus, Ali Mazrui is reported as a strong critic of the Non-Proliferation Treaty:

> "From a third world point of view, I don't believe the Treaty is worth the paper it is written on. And if I were to become President of a third world country, I would not hesitate to withdraw from it. Imperialism in the nuclear age is the monopoly stage of nuclear technology."[32]

Mazrui foresees an alliance of black South Africa with Nigeria and Zaire, which would develop its own African "deterrent".

> "Africa under its triumvirate of diplomatic leaders, partly endowed with nuclear credentials, will have begun to enter the main stream of global affairs. And the world as a whole, once it discovers the lunacy of its nuclear ways, will have learned an old lesson in a new context: the lesson that wild mushrooms are dangerous."

Of course, the attitude of the Government of Free South Africa cannot yet be determined. Fortunately, for many years, progressive people throughout the African continent have given their support to the goal of a nuclear-free zone in the whole region. Kwame Nkrumah froze all French assets because of the tests in the Sahara desert during 1961. At the same time, Nigeria severed its diplomatic contact with France. The advent of the Non-Proliferation Treaty was perhaps more keenly welcomed in Africa than in any other sector of the globe. Ogunbadejo believes that only a major initiative towards nuclear disarmament by the great powers can maintain this kind of wider global commitment.

"In the maintenance of future world order, the close co-operation and understanding between the superpowers and the other states with nuclear weapons is an essential precondition."

The advent of the Gorbachev - Reagan summits, and the conclusion of a Treaty to dismantle intermediate nuclear forces, welcome though it is, nonetheless arrives after the eleventh hour, when we consider the savage implications of the problems of proliferation. Conventional theories of deterrence are deeply flawed, and nowhere more than in their standard presumption of a bipolar model of nuclear confrontation.[33] In a crude way, several thousand warheads may, when confronted by several thousand other warheads, determine a certain kind of behaviour. No such determination may be presumed, however, once proliferation has extended to the "pariah" states. In the hot spots which include and surround these states, there is sufficient turbulence to encourage the insane idea that nuclear weapons can be useful as means of actual warfare. What elsewhere would be normal restraints of public opinion are here conspicuously absent. We have more than a little evidence that neither domestic nor international law controls the potential responses of such governments.

In small things, the Israeli Government kidnaps its opponents, and visits exemplary repression upon them. In large things, it misleads the United Nations and extends the threat of nuclear destruction to two of the most dangerous areas in the contemporary world.

It is hardly surprising that good people who are facing such threats may flinch in their commitment to oppose all or any reliance on nuclear weapons. Thus, Ogunbadejo tells us:

"Edem Kodjo, the last substantive Secretary-General of the

Organization of African Unity, caused quite a stir at the 19th summit during June 1983 in Addis Ababa, when he militantly urged African Governments to match "South Africa's nuclear mights": "it is the duty of member states which are able to resolutely embark on the nuclear path to do so." "[34]

Nuclear proliferation is the tragic *reductio ad absurdem* of deterrence theory. That old cynic, Harold Macmillan, cogently expressed the problem:

"If all this capacity for destruction is spread around the world in the hands of all kinds of different characters - dictators, reactionaries, revolutionaries, madmen - then sooner or later, and certainly, I think by the end of the century, either by error or insanity, the great crime will be committed."

The Non-Proliferation Treaty, and the idea of nuclear-free zones, can neither of them continue unaffected by the nuclearization of the military forces of Israel and South Africa. If there is still time to maintain the civilized commitment of Africa and the Arab world to non-nuclear defence policies, it must be evident that the time is rapidly speeding away. Mordechai Vanunu has removed the last veil which had been concealing this ugly situation.

Now, in order to survive, the Non-Proliferation regime must discover how to disarm Israel and South Africa of their nuclear bludgeons. A failure to confront this intransigent issue may not at once create the field full of dragon's teeth which will eventually grow. Problems of resources and technology will ensure an uneven development of nuclear military potential. But here, we are talking about something more fundamental than budget allocations: at stake is the whole question of the political will for peace and disarmament, as well as the deep-rooted problem of social justice. If the rest of the world abandons the front-line states to South African intimidation, including nuclear intimidation, all Africa will conclude that Ali Mazrui is right. If everyone outside the Middle East remains deaf to the process which is now reopening behind locked doors in Jerusalem, then the call for an Arab bomb will become irresistable. We are members of one another, and it is at critical moments like the present that it becomes necessary to demonstrate this fact.

So widespread is the international movement for peace, that the Third United Nations Special Session on Disarmament will see continued healthy pressures for the destruction of nuclear weapons, and the extension of ever-wider nuclear-free territorial agreements. Yet, it seems to me, that all these events provide us with a powerful argument that disarmament can no longer be left to governments.

There are widespread debates about the need for reform of the United Nations system, and many new proposals are emerging from the different peace movements, as they experience the weaknesses and limitations of the inherited UN system. Even within the old system, however, many voices have been raised for the creation of a new information order, as a pre-condition for an enlightened and active world public opinion.

The confrontation between Israel and its neighbours, the plight of the Palestinian people, and the abscess of apartheid are both major parts of a global crisis of militarism. This is worsening as a result of economic crisis, contraction and collapse. If the Stock Exchange crash leads through trade wars to the explosion of the world's debt bomb, then the present proliferation of nuclear weapons is a perfect formula for Armageddon. No-one can tell where conflict will spill over, once any of these sinister devices are detonated.

So urgent is this problem that nothing less than a world-wide popular movement is needed to meet it. It cannot be left to the immediate victims of these new nuclear threats, to protest and appeal in isolation. "Send ye not", said our English poet John Donne, "to know for whom the bell tolls: it tolls for thee".

*   *   *

In warning us of these perils, Mordechai Vanunu has earned our support and help. Writing from his confinement, he sent me this inspiring message:

"I hope you received my last letters to you. Last week I received the autobiography of Bertrand Russell. Thank you very much. In this very interesting book I find I share some things in common with the life of Russell. I am also governed by unbearable pity for the suffering of mankind.

I believe many people would like to do more for those who suffer without reason, like all the refugees in the world. I tried to help them when I was a student. This activity guides me to my next action.

Even now in these inhumane prison conditions, I feel good, because I believe I did my duty and followed my conscience.

I am happy to know that many people support and understand what I did, and my hope is that more people will do more things to stop nuclear proliferation throughout the world.

We are now in a great moment when the US and the USSR are signing an agreement to reduce nuclear weaponry in Europe. This is a good step in the right direction: to destroy all the nuclear weapons in the world.

I want to thank you for your action for peace, and for spreading news of my case to more people."[35]

I do not think that humanity will ignore or forget the plight of this good man. In organizing solidarity with him, we shall continually remind the world of the menace against which he warned.

Footnotes

1. The full text of this proposal was published in the *Guardian* in July 1987. After widespread international protests, the custodians of the prison in Jerusalem agreed to permit very limited visits by Vanunu's relatives. But Meir Vanunu was himself threatened with imprisonment, when he revealed, in the British press, the circumstances of his brother's abduction from Rome.
2. Israeli Statement: *The Iraqi Threat - Why Israel had to Act*, 7th June 1981.
3. Statement by Mr. Shamir to the General Assembly of the United Nations, 1st October 1981.
4. *Sunday Times*, 5th October 1986.
5. Ibid.
6. *Christian Science Monitor*, Israel Accused Anew of Nuclear Violations, by E.A. Wayne, p.32, December 2nd 1987.
7. United Nations: *South Africa's Plan and Capability in the Nuclear Field*, New York, 1981.
8. Robert F. Harkavy: *Spectre of a Middle Eastern Holocaust: The Strategic and Diplomatic Implications of the Israeli Nuclear Weapons Programme*, Kalamazoo, 1976.
9. Jane Hunter, *Israeli Foreign Policy*, Spokesman 1987, pp.35-37.
10. Adams, The Unnatural Alliance, p.170.
11. Speech to South African Institute of International Affairs, Johannesburg, September 13, 1986, Ibid., p.171.
12. Ibid., pp. 180-181 and p.195, which names the journalists as Eli Teicher and Ami Dor-on on their government sources.
13. "Halting Pretoria's A-test", *Newsweek*, September 5, 1977.
14. "A Friend in Need".
15. Walters, *The September 22, 1979 Mystery Flash*, p.1.
16. Ibid., p.5.
17. Ibid., p.16.
18. Ibid., p.1.
19. Jack Anderson, "U.S. Knew in Advance of Mystery Blast", *Washington Post*, April 26, 1985 and another column in *Washington Post*, September 14, 1980, Ibid., p.12.
20. Thomas O'Toole, "South Africa Ships in Zone of Suspected N-Blast", *Guardian*, January 31, 1980, Ibid., p.12.
21. Stephen Talbot, "The Case of the Mysterious Flash", *Inquiry*, April 21, 1980, Ibid., p.16.
22. Executive Office of the President, Office of Science and Technology, *Ad Hoc Panel Report on the September 22 Event*, July 15, 1980, Ibid., p.5.
23. Thomas O'Toole, "Neutron Bomb Suspected in Africa Blast", *Washington Post*, March 9, 1980, Ibid., p.7 and passim.
24. Thomas O'Toole and Milton Benjamin, "Officials Hotly Debate Whether

African Event was Atom Blast", *Washington Post*, January 17, 1980, Ibid., p.14.
25. Ibid., p.15.
26. Stephen Talbot, "The Case of the Mysterious Flash", *Inquiry*, April 21, 1980, Ibid.
27. "Evidence shows S. Africa tested A-bomb in '79", Reuter, *Jerusalem Post*, May 22, 1985.
28. Judith Miller, "2 in House Withdraw Atom Curb," *New York Times*, December 9, 1981 in Feldman, Israeli Nuclear Deterrence, p. 226.
29. Walters, *The September 22, 1979 Mystery Flash*, p.2.
30. Ibid., p.17.
31. Oye Ogunbadejo: *Africa's Nuclear Capability, The Journal of Modern African Studies*, 22,1, (1984) pp.19-43.
32. Ali Mazrui: *The African Condition, A Political Analysis*, London, 1980, pp. 122, 138.
33. In this connection, some of the remarks of General Secretary Mikhail Gorbachev are deeply significant. Cf, for example, his statement *Preserving Human Civilisation*, delivered at the forum in the Kremlin on February 16th 1987, and republished in ENDpapers No.15, Spokesman, 1987.
34. Ogunbadejo, op cit. p.25 Cf *Africa now*, August, 1983.
35. Mordechai Vanunu, letter from prison, *Morning Star*, 9th October 1987.

4

Peace, Rights and Freedom

Better dead than ... ?
Gathering in Japan to commemorate those who perished in the first nuclear explosions at Hiroshima and Nagasaki, we were in 1985 compelled to add the name of Chernobyl to our deliberations. Chernobyl was not a deliberate act of policy, but an accident. As an accident, it was greatly less serious than it might have been, and certainly less serious than it would have been, were it not for the supreme courage of those Soviet firemen who prevented the spread of conflagration from one reactor to the others, at the cost of their own lives. In spite of great organizational efforts, the after-effects of this disaster will endure, and remove from circulation lands and amenities which have been polluted to more lethal effect than the territories of Hiroshima and Nagasaki. Mankind is deeply worried by the warnings we have received from Chernobyl, no less than by the terrible warnings which were detonated in the Japanese skies in the first half of August 1945.

As Mr. Gorbachev told us during his broadcast after the Chernobyl events, we have been given a reminder of the awful finality of nuclear war.

Bertrand Russell used to claim that human beings could seek protection from adversity in one of two ways: there was the East Asian method, of the Chinese, who fought the floods by building dykes along the Yellow River: and there was the West Asian method of Noah, who "thought that the best protection was a virtuous life". Gradually, the

Chinese point of view has come to prevail, and people are more and more concerned to tackle their problems by relevant action, informed by thought. None the less, Russell was not wrong to conclude that "a virtuous life is as necessary to survival as dykes".

The Chernobyl plant was built close to major centres of population. Many ecologists, following the "Chinese" viewpoint, advocated that it should have been constructed elsewhere, very far from population centres. Let us imagine that this had happened. From where, then, would the courageous firemen have come? Because people lived near to the hazard, they were able to deal with it. If the plant had been in the frozen north, hours away from the necessary human intervention, then the disaster could have been many hundreds of times worse. This is no strong argument for building all new reactors close to population centres. Instead, it should persuade us that Noah was not wrong to seek his answer in a virtuous life. Rational anticipation of danger will only help so far: beyond that point, the choices are of a different kind. The choice about nuclear energy is not one of where best to locate its perils, but of whether they should be unleashed at all.

Almost no-one argues in favour of unleashing nuclear war. By now the empirical scientists have persuaded nearly everyone of the truth of the hypothesis of "nuclear winter". A very small exchange of nuclear weapons offers the risk of fundamental climatic change, which could eliminate the species, never mind the people who survived the blast and fallout of the next major war. That small handful of zealots who still put their trust in war have offered us a slogan, old but still heard in some places, "Better dead than red", they say. In Russell's time, an effort was made to invert this slogan and foist it on the peace movement. Attempts were made to typecast Russell as the spokesman of "better red than dead". He refused this role. First, he pointed out that the death involved in previous wars had claimed its victims from combattant generations. But death in the next war would prevail over all human posterity. It might be thought noble for a man to lay down his life in protection of his children, or the way of life of his peoples: it could not be so considered for a man to lay down the lives of his children's children, and their ultimate descendants.

Since a fullstop to human evolution cancels the possibility of victory for anyone, argued Russell, "it follows logically that a negotiated detente cannot be based on the complete subjection of either side to the other, but must preserve the existing balance while transforming it from a balance of terror to a balance of hope. That is to say, co-existence must be accepted genuinely and not superficially as a necessary condition of human survival".

How far, then, does co-existence imply the acceptance of injustice? Is it possible to found survival on morally acceptable principles? This is the question which has aroused considerable attention in the revived anti-nuclear movement of the 1980s. Of course, different sections of this vast movement give different answers: and indeed many individuals are not sure, themselves, how to answer. The issues are complex. Peace is more, we are often told, than an absence of war. But justice is also more than conformity with old rules, and people's expectations are constantly changing.

A classic problem of this kind emerged when on December 13th 1985, an international congress of intellectuals met in Warsaw at the invitation of the Polish authorities. The agenda was to consider the problems of peace and disarmament. A variety of

Polish oppositional organizations addressed an appeal to those visiting their country: it carried the title, *Peace and Freedom are Inseparable*.

The Polish opposition stated a number of justifiable complaints. The independent trade union movement, Solidarnosc, with ten million members, had been outlawed, and many of its leaders detained. Numerous independent social organizations had been disbanded at the same time. In spite of efficient and rigorous repression, however, such organizations continue to operate in Poland clandestinely. So the statement of the oppositionists proclaims "You have come to a country in which there is no peace".

In the same way, there is certainly no peace in South Africa. Central America knows no peace. There is no peace in Afghanistan, Kampuchea, Eritrea, or any of the other zones of conflict and civil war. While no-one thinks such wars should be fought with nuclear weapons, there always remains a risk that they could spill over to embroil nuclear powers, and thus "escalate". Injustice, wherever it is found, invites resistance and retaliation. Few among those living in happier circumstances would withhold their sympathy from such rebellion, even though it is overhung by Hiroshima, the shadow of which never leaves us.

The Polish authorities might be genuinely distressed to figure on such a list of oppressions as this. They did not choose their geographical location and would doubtless insist that their effort to promote discussions on peace were part of a more sustained effort to improve detente, and thus establish a more secure space for independent action. Indeed, it is entirely arguable that Poland's continuing present crisis resulted directly from the efforts of previous Polish governments to secure greater freedom of action within the Soviet sphere of influence. Why, other than to buy a degree of economic independence, should Polich ministers have borrowed so indiscriminately from Western banks? After the world oil crisis, such banks were desperate to lend to Governments, and particularly to Communist Governments which were thought to be among the safest potential recipients of funds. This was a miscalculation on both sides. Solidarnosc itself emerged in those Polish ports which experienced most directly the resultant trauma. In a desperate effort to meet spiralling inflation interest repayments, more and more frenzied efforts were made to export anything that would sell. Polish port workers found themselves cramming every ounce of meat into export-bound holds, while their wives would queue for hours for a tiny piece of sausage. Poland most assuredly undergoes a crisis which is both economic and political, and there are serious problems in her relationships with the Soviet Union. But these are not the only problems she faces. It was not the banks which banned Solidarnosc, even if they did precipitate the social crisis in which it was born. Those of us who are trade unionists, operating with greater or lesser degrees of freedom outside Poland, will all deplore the suppression of Poland's independent unions, and want to express our sympathy and support for their political prisoners. It is not surprising that the decision to outlaw the trade union has deepened the difficult situation in which the Polish Government operates. No doubt, among the ten million people who had organized themselves in Solidarnosc, there will be sufficient numbers of active spirits to continue their agitation. The more that such agitation brings down further repression, the truer it will be to say that there is "no peace". Even in countries where repression has been more effective, like Czechoslovakia, injustice and intolerance invite criticism and opposition. No-one should be reconciled to cynical usurpation. Does this mean, then, that there can be no co-existence?

Detente as an agency of human rights

Surely not. The struggles of Polish workers are in no way undermined by the existence of relatively normal relations between Poland and other states. If there is a detente in progress, then foreign journalists will be present in Poland, while Polish journalists are also stationed overseas. The more freedom such journalists experience, the more information will be spread about the state of opinion inside Polish factories. The more trade and cultural exchange there is, the more channels of effective communication there will be. Detente does not at all imply support for the Polish Government in its relations with its own people, and still less does it imply endorsement of repression and tyranny. It is arguable that the most propitious conditions for tyranny are those of isolation. The less a country interacts with the wider outside world, the worse its leaders can behave. The more direct material benefits a Government receives from international contact, the more reluctant it will be to put them in jeopardy. Of course, if tyrannies cross the bounds of civilized behaviour they may arouse moral revulsion which can produce the demand that they be ostracized. But here, we are dealing with a process. How difficult it is may be understood by looking at the case of South Africa, where rules an institutional racism, under which an overwhelming majority of people suffers the most systematic denial not only of its human rights, but of humanity itself. Yet it has taken decades of agitation to begin to isolate this system from the rest of the world polity.

Moral ostracism does not fall from the sky. People have to be persuaded that certain Governments are insupportable, that their tyranny is inexcusable and that it is necessary to take steps to boycott it. Commonly, such persuasion not only takes a long time, but only comes about as a result of strenuous efforts and intensive organization. Paradoxically these are helped throughout the interim by "normal" contacts.

Most authoritarian governments in the world are not complete tyrannies and are capable of movement in better or worse directions. If, in the absence of critical pressure, they are prone to lock people up, then, under such pressure, they may become more or less prone to let them out. Opposition to tyranny is a continuous process, a prolonged struggle.

In the same way, the struggle for peace is a continuous process, as is the campaign for nuclear disarmament. It would be extremely convenient if all these good causes ran along parallel tracks to an ultimate and harmonious destination. That, however, is not our experience. Some of the countries with very good policies on nuclear disarmament have somewhat bad histories of disrespect for human rights. Other countries with relatively good records on human rights at home have appalling records about disarmament. Just as disarmament negotiations involve elements of chicanery, deceit and gamesmanship, so the international argument on human rights is neither disinterested, nor is it always honestly conducted. There are many countries in which it is almost obligatory to disapprove of repression in Chile, but where the invasion of Czechoslovakia is always whitewashed. There are other countries in which the sufferings of Polish trade unions can be fully reported, but where such dreadful facts as the genocide in Timor are almost totally unknown and unreported. Selectivity in the news media is only part of the difficulty. Governments weigh in to deliberate effect. Thus, in the United States, after the debacle of Vietnam, President Carter unleashed a major "human rights" offensive which had two edges. First, it represented a reorientation of American policy within the US sphere of influence. From now on American officials were to distance themselves from the bloodiest dictators in Latin America, and to give greater comfort to centrist political forces. Secondly, towards the Soviet bloc, criticism of breaches of civil rights were to become part of a more political style of negotiation, pressing home every propaganda advantage which could be derived from the political weaknesses of the adversary. However, human rights were a boomerang when they were used as a weapon in the conflict between superpowers. Spheres of influence may have been easier to manage in the days of the old empires, when democratic expectations were minimal; but the rise of such expectations renders subject nations turbulent and client governments unstable. The election of President Reagan gave a savage blow to the United States campaign for "human rights": but this strategy of President Carter was already plainly collapsing even before the fall of his administration. Noam Chomsky has given us a magisterial description of the way in which this policy was dissembled, and of its cynical evasion of responsibility for consequences it had been designed to produce.

Peace and Freedom are linked. How to link the struggles for them?
The majority of members of governments are normally, most of the time, as concerned for the maintenance of peace as are peace movements

themselves. But the methods of governmental action necessarily base themselves on what is often miscalled "realism". Governments build dykes. In flagrant contrast, the idealism of peace movements, seeking salvation through virtue, can sometimes be represented as "unrealistic". Bertrand Russell, for instance, was a convinced advocate of world government. This is a perfectly logical proposal, and one which would imply the development of frameworks in which a whole series of more or less inter-connected problems might be solved in an orderly fashion. However, the majority of political leaders in the contemporary world still regards Russell's thinking on this matter as profoundly "unrealistic". This means that there is no single forum with the decisive power to determine the enforcement of human rights, or the level of international policing (and armament) that is consensually supportable. There are innumerable other problems which also lack solution in the absence of such a framework.

Among prime causes of conflict and war, we may list a few: the inequality of economic development between north and south; the effects of intensive competition between developed countries; slump, and the aggravated increase of enforced idleness among relatively highly skilled populations in "advanced" countries, as well as among the poorest; ecological imbalances resulting from avaricious exploitation of nature; the recurrent reappearance of famine and social distress. Mankind is not without considered strategies to face these problems. In June 1986, for instance, the Socialist International, gathering in Lima, adopted a most far-sighted report entitled *Global Challenge* and pledged itself to join action for its implementation. It remains to be seen whether Socialist Parties in the different countries are able to co-ordinate their activities on the relevant large scale. What is perfectly clear is that joint action between countries is all the more necessary in the absence of an accepted supranational authority.

Being "realists", perhaps this is as much as we can anticipate. But the human conscience is always unrealistic, and peace movements tend to see over the fences separating nations, to a wider world community. However, the lack of any global authority with power to act on all these issues simultaneously serves to do more than simply inhibit successful reform. It also separates the agencies of change, and compels the subdivision of the objectives of change. Of course, we all truly live in one world. We all truly desire peace in the world, and freedom, and the prospects of satisfying personal development for each individual among our people. But to bring more than a hundred governments into line to secure even the smallest step towards disarmament, requires a major campaigning effort. It is not easy to coordinate the efforts of 30 different peace movements, or trade unions. Since each of these organizations acts on its national plane, it evolves its overriding national priorities. Democracy, to the extent that it exists, operates at that national level and reinforces the partial view. National action is practical, step by step, "rational" and of course, limited.

Peace and human rights, jobs and freedom, these abstract goods are threatened in a crisis which results directly from uncontrolled competition within a system of separate political authorities. To overcome this separation, and obtain the joint action which is necessary, we quickly learn that we must separate our issues, focusing all possible attention on the most precise pressure points. For peace, we do require disarmament, and above all nuclear disarmament. It is easier to agitate against "the bomb" than it is to change the economic world, and remove the causes of slump, unemployment, and military competition. And yet all of us can perceive, and clearly, that the arms race correlates with economic crisis, and aggravates it all the time.

What, then, can we do? Separate national peace movements will not be able to evolve policies for the abolition of hunger and oppression, without taking on the duties of full-fledged political parties. Usually they will find it easier to persuade existing political organizations to address such issues, than it would be to elbow aside all established organizations. For the foreseeable future, peace movements will still need to prioritize their chosen goals, and to maximise pressures to the best of their ability. All this argues for a further development of international contact and exchange, as one necessary counter to the problems of specialization. And yet, there are other international pressures, which have already ensured that we have international organizations for human rights, international attempts at economic co-operation and a new international economic order, and international campaigns against hunger and poverty. Are we not arriving at the time when there needs to be some exchange between these separate initiatives? Is it premature to suggest that we should reach out towards one another, to knit together our efforts, not only to prevent the world from destroying itself, but also to render it fit to live in?

World government may be a long haul, and a difficult one to achieve. But we do have already an organization of United Nations, bringing together diplomats representing each separate state. The intermediate project which we need to match this dialogue of governments, is surely a United Peoples Organization, in which all the peace movements and social organizations can begin to refine the linkages which can form world public opinion, and make it effective.

If the United Nations were to move towards a more integrated structure it would probably seek to establish two chambers for its deliberations: one consisting of governmental representatives, as at present; and the other consisting of persons chosen in a process of direct elections.

Such proposals are seldom ventilated at the present time: although there are many people who would support them, and it cannot be doubted that they would help the development of relevant pressure groups. In the meantime, we have to make do with a growing network of non-governmental organizations. Everything which enlarges the scope for international democratic action helps to knit the world together. But the struggle for peace with human rights remains most active at the national level, in separate national territories, albeit with varying degrees of moral support from outside.

The most efficient globalism in the modern world has been established in completely non-democratic organizations. The giant transnational corporations extend their influence around the world, with cavalier disregard for the natural environment, and systematic indifference to humane social objectives. Frequently they are directly involved in political pressures to neutralize democratic decisions, wherever these might threaten profitable operations. Prominent among such corporations are the largest military producers. When accountable power has obtained a near-universal scope, it is at great peril that the democratic process restricts itself to partial, blinkered, separate national development.

5

European Nationalism and World Co-operation

The rise of nationalism in its modern sense owes everything to Europe, and if guilt were ever a useful response, we have every reason to feel guilty. If nation states were able to liberate economic forces for development, and to sponsor the growth of cultural identities, such states have normally pursued these goods by promoting an array of evils which have brought them into constant jeopardy. In our own century, these same evils prospered to a degree which brought the whole world into paroxysms of destruction.

The untold butchery of the First World War provoked and ensured the success of the Russian Revolution and consolidated the industrial power of the United States. As long ago as 1923, Bertrand Russell foresaw that this placed Europe in an unenviable dilemma:

> "there would seem to be two main possibilities, one the partition of Europe between Russia and America, the other the formation of a United States of Europe."

A partition, he stressed, would not necessarily annul all national choice in the states which were involved in it,

> "but ... each of these powers would be in economic alliance either with the West or with the East; and being unable to supply all their own needs, their diplomacy would have to be subordinate to one or other of their two great neighbours."

It is our desperate misfortune that the alternative

of unity in Europe was postponed indefinitely, and only became an option after a second holocaust had devastated the continent. The mechanisation of war had advanced to a level which rendered it unimaginably murderous. During the battle of the Somme alone, in 1916, 419,604 British, 194,450 French, and half a million German casualties were inflicted. Between 1939 and 1945, seventeen million combatants were slaughtered: but invention showed its continuous advance in the more significant fact that civilian deaths totalled even greater numbers.

The conflict of European nations spilled out across the entire world, and its victims were never adequately counted. Unnumbered millions perished in the Indian famine which withered the imperial province during the Second World War. The colonial legacy ensured recurrent wars in the aftermath, reaching horrendous kills in Korea and Vietnam, and draining lives in a whole series of independence wars in the French and British, not to mention the mutant American, Empires.

If this were the whole story, posterity would not easily forgive us. But of course, the growth of modern science and productivity was part of the same evolution, as was the painful evolution of democracy. In a remarkable paradox, democracy in Europe emerged very much the stronger after 1945, and there were important signs that at last the nations were beginning to learn. It was, however, too late to unite Europe, and partition had already come about before our politicians began to make tentative moves towards a degree of unity in the western half of the zone. While state legislatures were cautiously deliberating, however, convulsive changes were taking place in the economic structures over which they presided.

The growth of multinational corporations throughout the world had been the salient fact of postwar economic history. Such corporations drew strength from the Keynesian world settlement which determined a framework of monetary co-operation, and provided national governments with guidelines on economic regulation. Working within this settlement, careful demand management for a long time ensured the maintenance of full employment throughout most advanced economies over a period of decades. This not only created a degree of social harmony. The resultant long post-war boom ensured that the largest corporations entered upon a phase of truly remarkable growth and self-assurance. But these giant corporations, many of which were military producers, and which flourished precisely within the soil prepared by Keynesianism, steadily undermined the conditions within which they had come to prosper. Soon the existence of constellations of enterprises, straddling frontiers across the world, brought about the eclipse of nation states as economic controllers, regulators of growth and restraint. Once a company disposed of several plants in several countries, its internal trade enabled it to manipulate prices in such a way as to accrue surpluses in those places where trade unions were feeblest, and least demanding. The device of transfer pricing became endemic. Companies began to need not one but several sets of accounts, in order to follow their own internal progress, while at the same time placating national tax collectors, befuddling trade unions, and justifying claims on national state or local authority subsidies for economic rationalisation. A growing proportion of world trade came to consist in internal transfers within the large companies. Nation states which had sought to maintain levels of economic development which could guarantee employment, found themselves unable to do so, and were soon compelled to abandon the consensus politics of the post-war settlement. Instead they were pushed into seeking financial viability through a Dutch auction of interest rates, bidding one against the other for foreign funds, and causing an explosion of inflation. It is against the background of such troubles as these that the arms race roared away throughout the late 1970s and into our present decade.

Some economists believed, a decade ago, that the growth of multinational enterprise would quickly lever into being international economic organization on a matching scale. It was not difficult to imagine that the welfare states established in Britain, or Germany or France would ultimately be supplanted by a federal European machinery of welfare, as the separate capitals of Britain, France and Germany were merged and interlocked into a greater European capitalism. After all, the chemical industries, or electronics, require a high level of infrastructure in order to be able to operate effectively. Pharmaceuticals grow on the basis of developed medical services. All high technology industries require expanded and efficient systems of education. What could be more natural than that these institutions, which had become increasingly public systems during the first half of this century, should grow to become international agencies as the economy continued to develop? Such confident rationalism, alas, was not to prove well founded. The internationalization of markets was by no means followed through in an international development of welfare provision. As the great companies escaped from the more burdensome controls of national economic policies, they made no haste whatever to volunteer replacement contributions to effective social planning at an international level. Thus there arose a series of national crises in the infrastructures of education, public health and housing. And while the multinational corporations revelled in their new-found strength, the ghost of Adam Smith was raised in a modern parody of classical liberalism to justify still further weakening the capacities of nation states. Precisely at this juncture, international tension heightened to a new level of psychosis and a new arms race was launched. This made bids to erode still further the dwindling resources available for social care.

National Labour movements began to register alarm when it became clear that the rules of this competition implied, not the strengthening of their industrial base, but in some cases its actual disappearance.

Over the postwar decades, then, the growth of the power of transnational corporations has reached a point in which it has largely neutralised the macro-economic controls of medium-sized nation states, and thus devised a check on the evolution of national democracy as an institution. Loss of democratic control begins as a formal question, of the right to impose versus the power to avoid any particular decision. But with the effective collapse of the Keynesian world framework, we entered an era of mass unemployment which itself undermines social consensus, and deeply undermines the long-term stability of democratic institutions.

If, then, we may concede (with the reluctance we have been explaining) that there is a case to be argued in defence of nation states, to the extent that they have furthered democracy: surely we are bound to conclude that annulment of democracy would annul any remaining advantage to be found in this vestigial form of organisation. Our largest entrepreneurs have already established their preferences, for a sturdy cosmopolitan rationalism. Yet we remain caught in a tragic bind, because although economic power is now increasingly traversing frontiers, it remains, from the social point of view, entirely arbitrary and capricious, while the only available democratic mechanisms before which it might be brought to answer, are still almost entirely confined to the national level, where they are perceived as far too puny to be effective.

This circumstance occasions some real perils. Small though state powers may be to confront unemployment, organise economic recovery, build safe sewers, or maintain adequate systems of education and health, states everywhere do retain, and indeed commonly increase, prodigious spending powers. And by no means the least of these are in the military domain.

To chart present day economic competition is not the purpose of this discussion, and it is in any case a complex and difficult task. But if we consider three main centres within the present capitalist world, it is clear that the United States is exposed to effective competition from both Europe and Japan. Japanese progress has been, from this viewpoint, dauntingly successful. By 1990 Japan will have overtaken the United States as the world's most important holder of overseas investments. In key technologies, the Americans have begun to feel extremely threatened. If, in the world of robotics, optical fibres, lasers and communications technology, the Japanese maintain the initiative, then the whole process of tooling up for the 21st century will have been pre-empted.

No doubt this thought weighed extremely heavily with President Reagan when he was considering his Strategic Defence Initiative, or "Star Wars" programme. Seen at one level this is an unparalleled provocation to the Soviet Union, and a threat of runaway escalation in armaments competition. The thought of space lasers, powered by nuclear explosions, was fairly bizarre even when it was confined to comic newspapers. But if the President had sought to organize civilian investment in all those technologies which will shape the productive processes of the next century, such large scale government intervention would have been seen as communism, red in tooth and claw. As a military project, it is all explained as anti-communism, and therefore electorally acceptable.

The response of the socialist administration of France to all this was interesting. In announcing the call for Eureka, a European alternative to SDI, the French argued the need for sustained European investment in these communications technologies. At present, they said, Europe holds 15% of the world market in these techniques. Unless urgent action is taken, this share will decline to 10% by 1990. Were Europe to remain competitive throughout the world, it would need to expand to one-third of the total, rather quickly.

Here we arrive at a major difficulty. Eureka has been announced, of course, as a 'peaceful' collaboration. But Eureka, like the West European Union, grows in a space in which co-operation has been easiest: military co-ordination is politically far less contentious than civilian development. As things turn out, support for Eureka has been slow to materialize, and the American initiative has received such advantages in funding that already SDI is successfully recruiting European contractors while Eureka is still very much a controversy, at best a debate. In a far better way are the Japanese, who do not have to apply their minds to irrelevant military problems, but who can pursue direct responses to straightforward questions about civilian techniques. It will be surprising if this relative freedom from militarism does not ensure that the Japanese establish an accelerated lead in their chosen areas of skill.

A whole succession of other important economic issues have divided Europeans from the United States in recent years. There was the ferocious dispute about President Reagan's decision in June 1982 to prohibit European subsidiaries and licencees of American firms to trade components for the Euro-Soviet gas pipeline. There were keen quarrels about American protectionism in the steel industry. American monetary policies have been deeply disturbing to Europeans. A chasm yawned open between Europe and the United States on policy in the Middle East, because oil politics were in fundamental disaccord.

Europe shares interests which are sharply different from those of the United States on the flow of energy and oil supplies, and it is quite natural that this should become visible in reactions to a succession of Middle East crises, culminating in the scandal of the Libyan bombardment. General Bernard Rogers, NATO's Surpreme Commander in Europe, recently described the conflict on Libya between Europeans and Americans as worse than any he could remember. "He had never known as much antipathy within the Atlantic Alliance", reported *The Guardian*.

Europe also increasingly shares certain attitudes to East-West economic co-operation. The German Ostpolitik which survives in various forms in spite of changes in the West German political regime, is radically different from President Reagan's seige of the 'evil empire'. Increasingly it is clear that East Germany is a conduit for a vast access by the Soviet bloc to Western technologies. Relations betwen the two German states become more and more contingent upon this economic development. Of course, the resultant change produces effects which are felt both West and East of the Elbe. All these tensions between Europe and America are growing, and there is no reason, so far, to anticipate that they can diminish. What survives is a military alliance, and it is interesting that confrontation begins even within this. The development of the Western European Union seems to be about prospering European armament manufacturers rather than American based transnationals. The decision about the European fighter was quickly followed by a remarkable confrontation in Britain over the future of the Westland Helicopter Company. Here a consortium of European enterprises was quickly levered into existence in an attempt to fight off bids by the US Sikorsky combine. The accompanying political scandal revealed sharp disagreements between 'European' and 'Atlanticist' factions in the British Conservative Cabinet.

Up to now, all these tensions have been contained within the framework of the North Atlantic Treaty. But the flux continues to move. And the range of deep structured problems which have given rise to the Strategic Defence Initiative seem likely to produce shocks on an even greater scale than all these lesser collisions which have gone before. If the French Government is right about the steady competition of the Japanese, then the whole future of European based conglomerates comes into jeopardy. All the machine tools of the 21st century will depend on technologies such as those involved in SDI. Unless European research can be expanded on a geometric scale, there is small chance that such a project as Eureka could fill the gap in European know-how.

It is there that we should perceive a new relationship between the argument for economic autonomy and the argument for non-alignment. It is noticeable that European co-operation in production has been strongest in the military sector. Military investment is highly capital intensive, and creates far fewer employment opportunities than large civilian outlays. A modern bomber, verging on obsolescence, still costs 200 times the investment involved in bombers of the Second World War. When we look at straight-forward productive capacity, it is clear that while military appetites are virtually insatiable, the quality of products offered to the armed forces may be markedly variable. Huge sums of money are lavished on weapons systems which may be far from functional if they are ever deployed in actual battle.

But we are mainly concerned with the research function. It has long been argued that R and D for war production spills over into the civilian sphere. We are repeatedly informed that ballpoint pens have been given to us as by-products of military developments, or that Dowty Hydraulic Props in coalmines are the result of advances in military aviation. The American space programme has been given credit for originating non-stick frying pans, miniaturized pacemakers, lightweight sports equipment and new diagnostic techniques in hospitals. We are alleged to owe our jumbo jets to the evolution of military aircraft. In a recent study, Rockwell International identified some 30,000 secondary products which resulted from 27 years of work in the developing space programme. Of course, under President Reagan, the proportion of Research and Development expenditure allocated to defence has risen from about half to nearly three-quarters. If there were no "spin off" civilian development would be in a parlous condition. In fact, the notion that military research seeds civilian projects has become so popular that the powers risk a totally irrational approach to scientific enquiry. In my country, for long years, coalminers would go to work in military uniforms which had been cheaply sold off as surplus to requirements. This tradition goes back at least to the Boer War, and Osbert Sitwell has told us how, as a boy, he watched Derbyshire miners going off to work resplendent in scarlet tunics and greatcoats. A martian might believe that we needed an army in order to be able to manufacture cheap industrial clothing. In the same way, large numbers of earthlings believe that we need a war effort in order to learn how to refine transistors or microprocessors for gramophones or office calculators. But for such a level of insanity to enable us all to remain adequately crazy, all must share in it. The snag in the present madhouse is that one competitor, in Japan, remains infuriatingly sane. Spending less than 1% of their gross national product on military matters, the Japanese apply their research directly to the purposes for which they seek relevant solutions. They have discovered that it is cheaper to develop a digital watch by enquiring into the mechanics of digital watches: and that all that high-tech enquiry into targeting elaborate rockets to the other side of the moon is largely unnecessary in a watch factory. Accordingly, the United States bristles with Japanese goods. Computers, radio and television equipment, robotic devices, numerically controlled machine tools: the flood has already begun, and Noah Reagan has not yet commenced to build his ark. If, when he does, it is based on the assumption that it will only float if it is based on space technology, Mount Ararat will resound with

Japanese voices, not Texan ones, on the day after the waters subside.

Europeans must surely confront all these problems together. If a succession of disastrous wars have taught us the perils of nationalism, they have not yet shown us how to join our forces for peace. Economic co-operation has certainly developed, but it remains very much a reactive process rather than one of initiation. Think, for instance, what could be done in the promotion of electronics and communications research, if the whole of Europe's system of telecommunications were one transnational public utility. If certain such key economic sectors were effectively brought into government which was not only transnational, but also effectively socially accountable, it would be possible for them to be used to lever co-ordination and adaptation throughout the wider economy. Then alternative programmes of demand management by international governmental co-operation could become altogether more plausible. But while the cutting edge of European integration is a military edge, it will remain effectively blunt for all good purposes.

For sure, there needs to be a European defence capacity, and a European defence policy. But nobody is in a position to determine what these might be, until there is a European foreign policy, and a European peace policy at that. And we shall not know what these are until there is a European democracy which has the power to determine them. It is, however, in the highest degree unlikely that Europeans, approaching the twenty-first century, are wishing to emulate the two existing and declining superpowers. Unity offers other choices than ritual imitation, entry to the nuclear arms race, and foredoomed attempts to recreate old forms of domination and oppression. Unity, in any case, will never follow from the development of such an atavistic programme. It may not follow easily at all, but if it is to come, it will be as a result of rational discussion of an orderly agenda, in which both legitimate and disruptive contending interests may be recognised and either reconciled or overcome.

6

NATO and the International Court

On 27th June 1986, the International Court of Justice delivered its judgement against the most potent military power in the world.

The case against the United States of America had been brought by Nicaragua, which had suffered from continuous military and para-military onslaughts over a period of years.

There were 15 judges meeting under the presidency of the distinguished Indian jurist, Nagendra Singh. By 12 votes to 3, they decided "that the United States of America, by training, arming, equipping, financing and supplying the *contra* forces or otherwise encouraging, supporting and aiding, military and para-military activities in and against Nicaragua, has acted, against the Republic of Nicaragua, in breach of its obligation under customary international law not to intervene in the affairs of another state". The 3 dissenting judges, Oda, Schwebel and Jennings came from Japan, the USA and the United Kingdom respectively. The same 3 reaffirmed their dissent from a number of other crucial findings. By 12 votes to 3, the Court decided that the USA had infringed its obligations not to use force against another State by "certain attacks on Nicaraguan territory in 1983-4, namely attacks on Puerto Sandino on 13th September and 14th October 1983; an attack on Corinto on 10th October 1983; an attack on Potosi Naval Base on 4th/5th January 1984; an attack on San Juan del Sur on 7th March 1984;

attacks on patrol boats at Puerto Sandino on 28th and 30th March 1984; and an attack on San Juan del Norte on 9th April ". Again, by 12 votes to 3, the Court found that overflights of Nicaraguan territory, and the laying of mines in Nicaraguan territorial waters were actions contrary to customary international law and violations of sovereignty. The mining was also an interruption of "peaceful maritime commerce, and a breach of a 20-year of Treaty between Nicaragua and the USA". This last complaint found the solitary American judge alone in opposition.

Surprisingly, even the American judge condemned the United States for its failure to publish warnings about mining activities. American patriots might note that on this charge, the single dissenting judge was Oda, the Japanese. Oda it was, who further dissented from the finding that the USA "by producing in 1983 a manual entitled "Operaciones Sicologicas en Guerra de Guerrillas", and disseminating it to *contra* forces has encouraged the commission by them of acts contrary to general principles of humanitarian law". Whilst condemning the manual, the 14 judges felt that they were not entitled to impute to the Americans the responsibility for any actions which might subsequently be based upon its advice.

Again by 12 votes to 3, the Court decided that the United States trade embargo breached the 1956 Treaty of Friendship, Commerce and Navigation. The same more than adequate majority of judges concluded "that the United States of America is under a duty immediately to cease and to refrain from such acts as may constitute breaches of the foregoing legal obligations;" and more: "that the United States of America is under an obligation to make reparation to the Republic of Nicaragua for all injury caused to Nicaragua by the breaches of obligations under customary international law enumerated above".

Reparations were also due for injuries in breach of the Treaty of Friendship, Commerce and Navigation.

The International Court is the highest judicial body of the United Nations. It was established at the founding conference in San Francisco in 1945, and its statute formed part of the Charter of the UN. 47 States accept the compulsory jurisdiction of the Court in all legal disputes concerning not only the interpretation of Treaties and questions of international law, but also on the existence of facts which, if established, might breach international obligations. These states are also pledged to accept rulings on the nature of or extent of reparations for breaches of international obligations. Among the 47 are numbered both Nicaragua and the United States. In addition, several members of NATO have registered on this list. They are: Belgium, Canada, Denmark, Luxemburg, Netherlands, Norway, Portugal and the United Kingdom.

The United States, in initially accepting compulsory jurisdiction, reserved its position in respect of disputes arising under multilateral Treaties, unless all the parties to such Treaties were also parties in the case before the Court, or unless the American Government specifically signified its agreement to jurisdiction. But in 1984, the American Government reversed this decision and refused to recognize the competence of the International Court of Justice in the case brought against it by Nicaragua. The Court, in pressing on with its hearings, restricted its consideration of the dispute to those matters directly pertaining to the two parties before it, excluding claims involving multilateral Treaties, and thus honouring the original conditions under which the US Government had accepted its jurisdiction.

Of course, the Court's decision, from the moment of its announcement, could not avoid provoking reflection on certain very broad multilateral agreements. The most important of these is obviously the United Nations Charter itself. Chapter 1 of this Charter lays down purposes and principles, which include the commitment that all members "shall settle their international disputes by peaceful means", that all "shall refrain in their international relations from the threat or use of force against the territorial integrity or political independence of any State", and that "all members shall give the United Nations every assistance in any action it takes in accordance with the present Charter ... ". Although the International Court was ruling on a specific dispute, and in spite of the fact that it deliberately refrained from pronouncing on its implications for the UN, it is difficult to avoid the conclusion that its findings show that the United States has not been behaving consistently with the Charter. It might be argued that any contravention would be purged if the United States were to accept and implement the Court's decisions. But defiance of these decisions marks a qualitative deterioration in the case, and must surely from thence forward place the United States in a position of non-compliance with the Charter. American intervention might conceivably have been thought by some ill-informed persons (bizarre though this view must seem) to have been consonant with the UN Charter before the Court pronounced its judgements. But after that moment, until it came into compliance, there could be no doubt that the US Government was in fundamental conflict with the Court, and thus with the UN Charter itself, under which the Court was established.

It is at this point that other multilateral agreements are affected. Most significant of these is the North Atlantic Treaty, whose members have always claimed that they act strictly in accordance with the principles of the United Nations. Because, when NATO was created, the principle of universality involved in the United Nations was generally accepted by the peoples of both Europe and America, it was at that time unthinkable that any regional bloc should claim priority over the existing world-wide forum. For this reason, the preamble of the North Atlantic Treaty specifically reaffirms "faith in the purposes and principles of the Charter of the United Nations". Article 1 undertakes "as set forth in the Charter of the United Nations to settle any international disputes ... by peaceful means in such a manner that international peace and security, and justice, are not endangered, and to refrain ... from the threat or use of force in any manner inconsistent with the purpose of the United Nations". This is why members of the North Atlantic Treaty Organization must be thought to need and should require some explanations from the United States Government. As soon as the Russell Foundation obtained a copy of the judgement of the International Court of Justice it wrote to the NATO Prime Ministers about this matter. The questions involved were very simple. The first was "Do you believe that the North Atlantic Treaty should be observed by all signatories?" The second was "If so, what steps do you think might be appropriate to bring the United States of America into compliance with it?" The replies to these questions, and the more usual evasions of them, serve to tell us how far regional commitments have now down graded perceived obligations to the universal organisation.

On 21st July, Mrs. Thatcher's Private Secretary replied:

"The Prime Minister has asked me to reply to your letter of 8 July about the finding of the International Court of Justice in the case brought by Nicaragua against the United States.

The Court decided that it had no jurisdiction to rule on whether the US actions complained of by Nicaragua breached the United Nations Charter of other multilateral treaties. As you know, Article 1 of the North Atlantic Treaty simply reiterates obligations undertaken under the UN Charter.

I enclose a copy of the statement commenting on the ICJ judgement issued by the Foreign and Commonwealth Office on 27 June."

Mr. Powell enclosed an interesting memorandum from a Foreign and Colonial Office spokesman, which indicates that the British Foreign Office found the International Court's reasoning somewhat persuasive:

"FCO Spokesman: Friday 27 June, 2145 BST ICJ Judgement: US/Nicaragua

> 1. We have only just received the text of the judgement in this case. The Court has obviously considered the case very carefully and has reviewed thoroughly the evidence and facts presented to it.
> 2. The Court has now delivered a reasoned and detailed judgement. It is lengthy and will require careful study. Our reaction to it will reflect our adherence to the rules of international law which is fundamental to our foreign policy.
> 3. For many years we have accepted the jurisdiction of the Court and have invariably accepted its judgements in cases to which the UK was a party. We believe it plays a valuable role in international relations.
> 4. We note that the Court's decision is confined to customary international law and the Treaty of Friendship, Commerce and Navigation between the US and Nicaragua. We note that the Court was almost unanimous over its findings with respect to the Treaty and that there was a substantial majority with respect to customary international law."

In the light of the Foreign Office's reaction to the judgement, we did not find the Prime Minister's response totally persuasive, and we wrote again on 23rd July seeking further clarification:

"I received a letter from Mr. Powell, in reply to my own enquiry of the 8th July concerning the International Court's findings on the case of Nicaragua versus the United States.

Mr. Powell informs me that the Court decided it had no jurisdiction "to rule on whether the US actions complained of by Nicaragua breached the United Nations Charter or other multilateral treaties". This, however, is not the point. The Court was ruling about past behaviour, and it found that the United States "is under a duty immediately to cease" such behaviour, as well as to pay reparations for previous infractions. The question which affects the North Atlantic Treaty does not concern past behaviour, but future behaviour.

Refusal to accept a decision of the International Court of Justice, the principal judicial organ of the United Nations, is presumably to act in "a manner inconsistent with the purposes of the United Nations".

If the government intends to follow the guidelines laid down by the Foreign and Colonial Office spokesman on Friday 29th June, which you kindly passed on to me, then it is difficult to see how we can react in "adherence to the rules of international law" if we make no effort to enforce the terms of the North Atlantic Treaty, which will have been breached by a refusal to act upon the Court's decision.

Before that decision, the United States might or might not have been in breach of the Treaty, and as Mr. Powell rightly says, this matter was not resolved at The Hague. But things are quite different after the judgement, which presumably defines the attitude of the United Nations, since it represents the ultimate legal authority within that body. In short, how can one defy the International Court of Justice and observe Article 1 of the North Atlantic Treaty?"

On 4th August Mr. Powell replied on behalf of the Prime Minister, in the following terms:

"The Prime Minister has asked me to reply to your letter of 23 July about the International Court of Justice findings in the case of Nicaragua versus the United States.

Your views have been noted.

It has been a central plank of British foreign policy since 1949 to support the NATO Alliance. I can reassure you that this support will be fully maintained."

Evidently Mrs. Thatcher did not wish to discuss the issue further, since she made no effort to answer the questions. But neither did she contradict the arguments which gave rise to them.

Lord Carrington, the Secretary General of NATO, also replied in a somewhat defensive vein. On the 25th July he wrote:

> "I have given thought to your letter of 8th July in which you suggest that the International Court's recent ruling on certain issues raised by Nicaragua might also raise questions about U.S. compliance with Article 1 of the NATO Treaty.
>
> It would not be appropriate for me to comment in substance on the legal and political implications of the ruling of the International Court; but it may be worth recalling that the case was one in which the United States denied that the Court had jurisdiction, did not therefore present its side of the case, and maintains that its actions in Central America are fully consistent with U.N. principles and international law, particularly as regards assistance in cases of collective self-defence.
>
> As far as the North Atlantic Alliance is concerned, I think most people would find the linkage you propose rather artificial given the U.S.'s long-established and strong commitment to the NATO Treaty."

We answered on the 14th August:

> "Thank you very much indeed for your letter of the 25th July concerning the International Court's ruling on Nicaraguan complaints against the United States. As you know, the International Court is the highest juridical body of the United Nations Organiztion constituted under Articles 92-96 of the United Nations Charter. Prior to the Nicaraguan complaint, the United States had accepted its compulsory jurisdiction alongside 46 other States. Amongst these were Belgium, Canada, Denmark, Luxemburg, Netherlands, Norway, Portugal and the United Kingdom, all of whom share adherence to the North Atlantic Treaty. According to Article 92 of the UN Charter, the statute of the International Court of Justice "forms an integral part of the present Charter". It is therefore difficult to see how a State can defy a Court decision, and remain in conformity with Article 1 of the North Atlantic Treaty.
>
> Are you suggesting that it is "rather artificial" to expect that Treaties be observed? What is in question is not the United States commitment to the North Atlantic Treaty, but its obedience of the United Nations Charter. Of course, in the world of common-sense, many of us have long suspected that regional alliances such as NATO and the Warsaw Treaty do tend to displace loyalty to the United Nations Organization. But statesmen within these Alliances have always denied this. Have you reached the point where it can now be confirmed?"

It took some time before Lord Carrington replied, on the 9th September. He, too, did not wish to involve himself in any more discussion:

> "Thankyou for your further letter about the International Court's recent ruling on Nicaraguan complaints against the United States. I have nothing to add to what I wrote to you in July."

Perhaps he had already said too much, however. If it is the view of the Secretary General of NATO that the United States might be justified in denying jurisdiction to the International Court of Justice, and in refusing to present its side of the case, then isn't the North Atlantic Treaty Organization taking sides against the British Foreign Office, which adjudged matters very differently? The Foreign and Colonial Office may not have finished its "careful study", but its initial reaction of 22nd June sits uneasily with the idea that the International Court Judgement can simply be disregarded. In the beginning, at least, the Foreign and Colonial Office were obviously predisposed to take the Judgement rather seriously.

Some other NATO allies also preferred to reserve their positions. A letter to Chancellor Kohl along the same lines as that to Mrs. Thatcher, produced on 30th July this response from the German Foreign Office:

> "The Federal Chancellor has asked the Foreign Office to acknowledge receipt of your letter of 8th July 1986.
>
> The FRG is not a party to the conflict in Central America and did not take part in the proceedings mentioned by you before the International Court of Justice in The Hague. It therefore takes up no position regarding the details of the proceedings and the verdict of the Court.
>
> Besides, the Federal Government has always stressed that it advocates strengthening international organization and international jurisdiction and universality of civil rights. Its policy in Central America is orientated towards the basic aims of peace through dialogue and development through economic co-operation. In this the Federal Government is conscious of being in agreement with its European partners."

As if this might not be clear enough, a further response from Dr. Hellbeck, in the Foreign Office, was sent on the 13th August:

> "Thank you for your letter to the Federal Chancellor of 8th July 1986. The Foreign Office has been asked to reply.
> The content of the judgement of the International Court of 27th June is of course known to the Foreign Office. It was issued in a case brought by Nicaragua against the USA. The Federal Republic was not a participant in this case. There is therefore no reason for the Federal Government to comment either directly or indirectly on the result."

The problem with this response is not simply that it does not answer the question. Let us make an analogy with any similar action taking place in a national court, within national jurisdiction. Quite evidently, representatives of government could not possibly pronounce themselves to be indifferent to the enforcement of court decisions, simply because they themselves were not parties in a dispute. Cynics will tell us that the response of the German Government merely highlights the difference between national law and international law. International law, we are often told, is unenforceable. This may be strictly true, but attitudes to international law none the less reveal a very great deal about the direction and commitment of the authorities involved. It could certainly be argued that European governments need to take up a strongly supportive policy to the International Court of Justice, and to the wider question of the enforcement of international agreements and obligations. The countries in the European zone, which are seeking closer economic integration and association, cannot afford to be negligent on this matter. To profess oneself indifferent to the enforceability of an International Court decision, when it affects the conduct of one's close ally, is not very consistent with this need. European statesmen are likely, if they follow this trend, to find that they have greater and greater dependence on an enforceable framework of international law governing economic decisions, at the same time that their political alliances render international legalities more and more inconvenient.

Other Governments were more aware of this problem. On August 20th, Mr. A. J. Ettema, of the Dutch Ministry of Foreign Affairs, offered a very different kind of response:

> "In response to your letter of 8 July 1986 I wish to point out the following:
> The Netherlands attaches great importance to the principle of peaceful settlement of disputes and recognizes the important role of the International Court of Justice in this field. Accordingly it has, on a reciprocal basis accepted the compulsory jurisdiction of the ICJ and hopes that those states which have so far not done so, will also decide to recognize the Court's compulsory jurisdiction in the future. In the Netherlands view rulings of the Court in cases which fall under its compulsory jurisdiction and in other cases which have been laid before the ICJ should be honoured by the parties involved.
> With regard to the conclusion you draw from the Courts ruling, i.e. that the United States would be in breach of Article 1 of the North Atlantic Treaty as this article refers to the United Nations Charter, I would like to underline that the Court explicitly decided (by eleven votes to four) that it had no jurisdiction to adjudicate the dispute on the basis of the United Nations Charter."

This letter arrived in England while I was abroad so that I could not reply until the 9th September. Although the attitudes of the Dutch Government showed altogether greater concern for the International Court of Justice, I found it necessary to repeat a point I had tried to explain in the earlier correspondence with Lord Carrington and Mrs. Thatcher.

> "Thank you for your kindness in replying to my letter of the 8th July, concerning the International Court of Justice findings in the case of Nicaragua versus the United States. Of course I welcome

the position of the Netherlands Government on this judgement, and believe that this is an entirely proper response to the issues involved.

However, I think that I did not make clear the gravamen of my point about the United States breaching Article 1 of the North Atlantic Treaty. Of course, you are right about the position of the Court concerning its lack of jurisdiction to adjudicate the dispute on the basis of the United Nations Charter. Whatever we think about that decision it is now a given fact. But this had nothing to do with my complaint: which does not concern what happened before the Court reached its decision, but what has been happening since that time. If the United States Government had accepted the Court's findings, or even if it had agreed to comply with them, whilst continuing to dispute them in argument, then it might be argued that the United States remained in compliance with Article 1 of the North Atlantic Treaty. But the defiance of the International Court must surely constitute a breach of Article 1, since the International Court is the highest juridical body of the United Nations? In other words, the problem is not one over which the International Court needs to make any pronouncement: either the United Nations institutions are enforced, or they are not, and failure to enforce them contravenes the spirit of the Treaty.
Do you think this reasoning is fallacious?
I should greatly value your advice on this matter."

Two other Prime Ministers gave strong support to the International Court of Justice, and to its Nicaraguan judgement. From Norway, Eldrid Nordbø replied on behalf of the Prime Minister on the 9th September:

"The Prime Minister has asked me to thank you for your letter of 8 July 1986 about the judgement of the International Court of Justice concerning military and paramilitary activities in and against Nicaragua.

The Court has delivered a judgement based on sources of international law which it shall apply in accordance with its statutes. The Norwegian Government is firmly supporting the Court and believes that its role should be strengthened. At present the Government does not see any need for adopting a position on sources of international law, non-applicable or applicable, which are extraneous to the completed deliberations of the Court."

From Spain, Mr. J. Julio Feo replied on behalf of Felipe Gonzalez on 9th September:

"I'm pleased to acknowledge receipt of your kind letter of 8 July to the Prime Minister, and at the same time to express his appreciation of the task that the Foundation has been developing in favour of international peace and justice.

The Spanish Government's position regarding the Central America conflict is well-known and has been repeatedly demonstrated in every appropriate international forum, and lately in the debate which took place at Nicaragua's initiative in the Security Council. Our stance arises from the premise that international law and the principles contained in the United Nations Charter must be fully respected by every State. The need to respect them is particularly evident in conflicts which place in danger international peace and security. In these circumstances our best guarantee to find solutions is to abide by international law and to observe the principles of the Charter, according to the guidelines provided by the competent bodies of the United Nations.

The Spanish Government is firmly convinced that it is necessary to reach a full, regional, peaceful, and negotiated solution in Central America. In this spirit we continue to actively support the task that the Contadora Group has been developing for more than three years, and that, after the establishing of the Support Group, has come to represent the feelings of every Latin American democracy and has produced a strong response from the international community Within this same line the Spanish Government has been working, and will go on working, both in its contacts with those Governments directly involved and within the European Political Co-operation."

This international correspondence ceases with this statement. In the absence of further replies, we hope that other people will join us in pressing for answers. Of course, there are very many people who believe that States are completely cynical when they conclude Treaties, and that it is a matter of rather small consequence that such Treaties are violated. We are bound to accept that such violations happen, and that international law is not easily, and certainly not neutrally, enforceable. But this is not a situation we should uncomplainingly accept. The project for a United Nations Organization, properly understood, committed its protagonists to a long struggle for acceptable standards of international behaviour. In democratic countries, this struggle benefits from the active involvement of concerned citizens. It seems to us that people living in countries which have endorsed the North Atlantic Treaty should be encouraged to insist upon the enforcement of its firm commitment to the United Nations. Failure to pursue this question, surely, means compliance in illegality and growing international brigandage?

Certainly since the United States Government decided that it would not respond to Nicaragua's complaints to the International Court, we have seen a fierce escalation of violence in other areas. In Libya, to take only the most evident example, direct American action followed the unilateral Libyan declaration of territorial control over the Gulf of Sidra/Sirte. Neither this decision, nor even the more difficult question of allegations concerning international terrorism were matters beyond the reach of the International Court of Justice. Why did the Americans not seek recourse to this Court? Of course the main answer is very plain: repudiation of the Court's competence in one area is extremely difficult to square with assertion of that competence in another. Already the United States was in some difficulty, because it had enthusiastically (and understandably) welcomed the earlier International Court judgement in its own dispute with Iran, a few years earlier. Having now denied the relevance of international law to cover one problem, there followed an inexorable retreat to policies of force in another quite different and unrelated zone. These specific problems, of course, raise wider issues. In a world bristling with nuclear weapons, such issues are frightening to contemplate.

7

Reform of the United Nations

The only universal organization in today's world is the United Nations. Fifty-one states joined forces to found it in 1945, and year after year it has subsequently grown to its present membership of 159 states. This process of growth has reflected the erosion of the great European empires, and the success of the many movements for national independence in Africa, Asia, and Latin America. All this is a great achievement of mankind, and needs to be vigorously defended against its powerful detractors.

However, the United Nations General Assembly consists of diplomatic representatives of states, each of which carries one vote, regardless of the size of the population it may represent. During the earliest years of the UN, there were frequent discussions about the establishment of a directly elected Chamber for the Organization. Naturally, such a proposal raises great difficulties for the principle of national sovereignty, which was written into the founding principles of the new organization. The first of these principles insists on "The sovereign equality of all ... members". The last of them renders this specific by insisting that "nothing in the Charter is to authorize the United Nations to intervene in matters which are essentially within the domestic jurisdiction of any state".

When the League of Nations had been established, following the First World War, it constituted a response to a whole generation of pacifist and socialist advocates who had sought to establish conditions in which national interests might be arbitrated by a supra-national influence. Thus, during the war itself, which he consistently opposed, Bertrand Russell wrote:

> "If civilization is to continue, Europe must find a cure for this universal reign of fear with its consequence of mutual butchery. One way in which it might be cured is that the civilized nations, realising the horror and madness of war, should so organize themselves as to make it practically certain that no advantage can be gained by initiating an attack. For this purpose it would be necessary to avoid exclusive alliances and to form a League of Peace, which should undertake, in the event of a dispute, to offer mediation, and, if one party accepted mediation while the other refused it, to throw the whole of its armed support on the side of the party accepting mediation, while, if both parties refused mediation, the League should throw its weight against whichever party proved to be the aggressor."[1]

To this prescription was joined a denunciation of secret diplomacy and other ills which were associated with the outbreak of the 1914 conflict. The English historian A. J. P. Taylor, summarized all this very clearly:

> "Bertrand Russell provides a striking example. The final chapter of *The Foreign Policy of the Entente* laid down Radical principles of foreign policy: no annexations; renunciation of the right of capture; universal arbitration; no alliances or understandings; 'we shall not engage in war except when we are attacked.' Appended to this is a footnote: 'Unless a League of Great Powers could be formed to resist aggression everywhere ... In that case, we might be willing to participate in a war to enforce its decisions.' "[2]

Taylor mercilessly captures the contradiction in this commitment:

> "Woodrow Wilson himself did much the same, when he thought to change the character of the treaty of Versailles by tying the Covenant of the League to its coat-tails. Every advocate of the League weighed with two measures. Their books described at length the misdeeds of statesmen all over the world. Then, in a short final chapter, they assumed that the same statesmen would become persistently virtuous once a League of Nations had been set up."

This contradictory position was still continued after 1945, even if the disintegration, over some decades, of colonial empires, and the rise of non-alignment, offered hopes that things might improve. In the absence of higher authority, governments would usually exercise their sovereignty to defend their narrow interests. Some of the lessons of the weakness of the League of Nations were drawn by the architects of the UN. Thus the charter of the International Court of Justice was deliberately incorporated into the Charter of the UN itself.[3]

Resonant declarations accompanied the promulgation of the United Nations Charter in San Francisco during the summer of 1945. Speaking in a foreign affairs debate in the British Parliament, shortly after the election of the 1945 Labour Government, Anthony Eden, the Conservative spokesman, opened with one of these:

> "We have somehow to take the sting out of nationalism. We cannot hope to do this at once. But we ought to start working for it now, and that, I submit, should be the first duty of the United Nations ... I want to go to a world where the relations between nations can be transformed in a given period of time, as the relations between England, Scotland and Wales have been transformed."[4]

Such a transformation clearly implied intrusions into the principles of national sovereignty, as generations of Scottish and Welsh nationalists will readily testify. Bevin had to respond for the first time in his new role as Foreign Secretary in the Attlee administration. In what one of his biographers has called the "greatest speech of his life"[5] he went far beyond Eden to embrace Taylor's criticism of the arguments which Russell had espoused three decades earlier.

> "We are driven relentlessly to the necessity of a new study for the

purpose of creating a world assembly, elected directly from the peoples to whom the governments that formed the United Nations are responsible, to make a world law which the people will accept, and be morally bound to carry out ...

The common man is the great protection against war, and the supreme act of government is, after all, the horrible duty of deciding matters which affect the life and death of the people. That rests on the House of Commons as far as this country is concerned.

I would merge that power into the greater power of a directly elected world assembly in order that the great repositories of destruction and science, on the one side, might be their property, to protect us against their use, and, on the other hand, it could easily determine whether a country was going to act as an aggressor or not.

I am willing to sit with any body, any party, or any nation to try to devise a franchise or a constitution for a world assembly for a limited objective — the objective of peace."[6]

In spite of his enthusiasm for this utopian project, Bevin was soon to prove himself very much more agnostic about the actually existing organization of United Nations. His main biographer, Lord Bullock, chronicles a whole series of events in which Bevin showed himself keen to prefer national, and indeed imperial, interests over global ones.[7]

But the argument for an elected world assembly continued to develop. In 1953, two American lawyers, Grenville Clark and Lewis B. John, of the Harvard Law School, published a project on *Peace Through Disarmament and Charter Revision*.[8] They proposed a detailed solution to Bevin's constitutional problem. Each member state of the United Nations would be entitled to one representative for each five million of its electors, or major part thereof. There would be an upper limit of thirty representatives from any one state. States with less than two and a half million citizens would be represented by delegates with voice but no vote. Adjustments would be made as populations changed, within a maximum global representation of four hundred deputies.

Other proposals for a bicameral governing body, maintaining the existing General Assembly and adding a parallel Popular Assembly, were advanced by World Federalists and the World Association of Parliamentarians for World Government. From the University of Chicago came a proposal for continental electoral colleges to appoint members of a global parliament. This debate continued in a fairly lively state throughout the first postwar decade.[9]

But during all this time, the UN was falling far short of the status of universality. Numerous nations were excluded from membership. The most towering example of these was People's China, barred in 1949 and kept at bay until 1971. As the cold war raged, and nuclear weapons proliferated horizontally (somewhat) and vertically (a great deal), so the consolidation of blocs progressively stifled the striving for direct international popular representation.

The detonation of the first thermonuclear device provoked worldwide concern, and following the Russell-Einstein Appeal, directly engendered first the Pugwash Movement of scientists, and later a new popular movement for nuclear disarmament. Addressing this, Russell returned, in two books, to his old theme of world government.[10] Now, he sought a world legislature with the sole power to register and confirm treaties, and revise them if they conflicted with international law. This body would be able to object to "violently nationalist systems of education" if they appeared to constitute a danger to peace. It would sustain an executive with control of armed forces, of which it would hold a monopoly. And it would confer on the institutions of international law "the same authority as belongs to national courts".[11] In an early essay on the same theme, he advocated a transitional approach through conciliation to an international authority.[12] It is fair to say that these proposals attracted less serious attention than any of Russell's other arguments about the nuclear peril, developed at the same time, and indeed, in the same writings. Reform of the United Nations has never entirely disappeared from the agenda of political discourse, but it is difficult to deny that it has long ceased to attract widespread attention, or any degree of priority in public opinion.

Nonetheless, global integration was continuing, and rapidly continuing, by other means. The acceleration of colonial freedom movements continued in spite of frontal imperial interventions by the European powers and both overt and covert destabilisation by the American Central Intelligence Agency. Non-alignment became a power in the world. The doors of the United Nations could not remain for ever locked against this vast upheaval in the global system, and the organization became, by the beginning of the present decade, almost universally inclusive. It also began to make decisions which were unwelcome to authority in the most potent chancellories of the world.

At the same time, great political and economic changes were under way. There were always many obstacles to the surrender of national sovereignty to any supranational power, be it never so carefully conceived. Some of these obstacles reflected particular interests, and were shabby and sometimes exploitative. But perhaps the most important obstacle of all was not at all concerned with vested interests. It drew its force from the fact that it reflected progressive concerns and commanded support from all who were likely to listen to internationalist appeals. It was, of course, the fact that the conquest of democracy had either taken place at the national, state level, or not at all. Democratic power, in the postwar world, was national power, and therefore sovereignty was not merely linked with particular national interests, but also with a universal political aspiration, above all in the working populations, and among the most progressive political parties. Democratic power grew in the more economically developed countries with the establishment of the Keynesian world order, within whose framework prospered national economic management, regulation of demand, full employment, and strong, if usually subordinate, trade unions. In all such countries there arose a consensus of welfare and political balance. But the same economic order provided ideal soil for the growth of transnational corporations, within whose massive concentrations were gathered more and more of the world's production and trade, and ultimately the very real capacity to evade or nullify national state policies on the development of their economies.

National democracies, in short, soon began to face the pressures of an international economy, completely beyond their direct control. The world of the transnationals abrogated the age of Keynes, and confronted national governments with stark choices, all of which were increasingly incompatible with the postwar democratic balances. The same violent focussing of economic power burnt out even more damaging holes in the social fabric of the emergent nations, and engendered strong support for the call for a new international economic order.

But, however comprehensive the membership of the United Nations, its powers were nowhere near adequate to meet such a challenge. Indeed, the UN agencies most directly affected came under sustained criticism and attack. In the United States, a sinister organization called the Heritage

Foundation spent vast sums of money on campaigns against such bodies as UNESCO and the FAO, as well as funding onslaughts on the UN system as a whole. The Americans and some of their clients abandoned UNESCO. Mr Gough Whitlam, former Prime Minister of Australia, has given a laser sharp account of the orchestrated press-barrage in Britain, which, after an intensive burst of editorials and signed articles (in no fewer than thirteen newspapers during a single month of 1984) culminated in Sir Geoffrey Howe's announcement of British withdrawal on October 22. An excerpt from Mr Whitlam's indictment is featured as an appendix to this chapter. First the French and then the United States decided to ignore and then defy the International Court of Justice. Indeed, the wider the representativity of the UN, the more recalcitrant has been the conduct of international relations by the United States Government. In 1985 this conduct provoked strong admonitions from the Socialist International.

In 1987, the United Nations lives in a world which may, hopefully, be about to enter on the first tentative steps to nuclear disarmament. But however great the will to peace, the obstacles to that peace do not consist in arms alone, but rather in the conditions which promote the accumulation and use of arms. And what are these conditions? There is a worldwide crisis of indebtedness, in which whole families of nations find that their investment potential has been confiscated for years ahead. Structural problems of great severity afflict most 'advanced' economies even during times of relative upturn. Almost 20,000,000 people lack work in Europe. Recovery of full employment is far from the top of the agendas of those governments which have departed most considerably from it. If the United States goes ahead with plans to balance its budget which have already been mooted, European unemployment will rise again to some 24 million. The effects in the South will be catastrophic. Development in the South, and recovery in large areas of the North, certainly call for international co-operation in new ways, and offer the United Nations and its agencies much scope for action.

And yet the crisis of recovery and development remains a crisis of nation states, of national democracy, and of sovereignty. Unemployed people in Spain or the Netherlands want jobs in Spain and the Netherlands, not some abstract upturn which passes over their heads. The political impasse of the present crisis does not result from too much national sovereignty, but too little. National democracy has by no means been overtaken by accessions of powers to the UN, but bypassed and neutralised by arbitrary and unaccountable private economic powers. The most rigorous conservatives in Europe seek to solve the resultant problems, not by democratic advance in international co-operation, but by reverting to pre-democratic forms of laissez-faire, at any rate concerning the most potent corporations, actually abrogating or repealing those democratic powers which might be conceived to impede corporate aggrandisement.

In this painful world it is plain that democracy cannot simply jump over the states in which it has been confined. It is bound to seek to defend its national spaces, and to recover control over powers which have been filched from it. Today is not the day when democrats can afford to join in the lobby to annul rights which are proving all too difficult to preserve. And yet international co-operation, joint action between states and democratic agencies, becomes, increasingly, a prior condition for even the most limited success in the struggle against unbridled economic concentration.

Because such co-operation is not easy, it will be likely to emerge tentatively, and to be cautious in its initial scope. And because the development of the United Nations itself will be determined in this process, we must face up, at the same time, to two contradictory imperatives.

> One: national independence and autonomy must be upheld as still the most basic area of democratic advance.
>
> Two: the growth of transnational economic power, and the weight of accompanying crisis, demand measures of international co-ordination which can best be undertaken within a democratic framework.

The first principle of this argument is of course linked to the second. The national interests, and the democracy of Nicaragua or French Polynesia, for instance, would be well served by acts making International Court judgements enforceable. The linkage works also in reverse, however, because the resistance of those powers found culpable in such actions as these spills over to inhibit their co-operation even in areas in which their own interests might obviously benefit.

All these considerations may combine to persuade us that the time is not yet propitious for us to tackle the agenda set up by Russell, or by Bevin in his headier moods. States will think it ill-advised to surrender still more of that competence they precariously retain, constantly eroding as it is in an unfriendly economic environment. On the contrary, they will be likely to seek, in their international actions, to recover power and sovereignty, and to regenerate democratic influence, precisely in order to address their domestic crises more effectively.

Yet the existence of a universal international forum is too precious an asset to be ignored in this process. There is a stronger case than ever before for direct elections to a United Nations popular assembly, provided we pitch it at the right level, addressing the problems involved in it realistically, and aiming for as much as will be seen to be useful at the present juncture.

What functions should be addressed in such a case? The answer seems very plain. It is at the level of world public opinion formation that the present United Nations system is weakest. Widespread international action can be mobilised on specific issues, such as opposition to Apartheid, or relief of famine: but the movements engaged in these causes usually emerge spontaneously, without directly impinging on the United Nations until they have already become strong; while there remain numerous urgent questions about which even informed pressure groups within different countries act in isolation, without forming the very linkages which could be decisive in the presentation of their arguments. If there were a UN popular consultative assembly, it would perform major services even were it to exercise no physical powers whatever. First, supposing in the modern age that every six million adults in the world were to be invited to choose a representative for such a world forum, this could imply a process of election in which all the key issues would be extensively discussed. Parties would gell to express the different options, and many concealed issues would be opened up. The press and television services would shift their attention, for a vital if brief period, to a global agenda. Second, national democratic forces would quickly discover their most appropriate international partners in dialogue and joint action. Linkages would emerge quickly and by rational choice rather than haphazardly and in the light of restricted and sometimes false information.

Thirdly, the received perceptions of national interest would face both internal and external scrutiny. Fourthly, even the most limited assembly would become a focus for a thousand lobbies and causes, and a sounding board for all the innumerable non-governmental agencies. Lastly, by expanding the concern of the peoples for the United Nations, we would ensure that all the reactionary and fissiparous lobbies against it would receive a decisive rebuff.

Of course, such a consultative body could be constituted with no power, little power, or somewhat more. Beginning with a procedure in which conventions might be adopted to express the majority view, it might follow the example of the International Labour Organization, and monitor and encourage ratification and enforcement of such conventions by responsible governments. Moving further, it might exercise a range of influences within the specialised agencies. At a higher level, it might begin to discharge some of the functions which used to be argued by reformers in the 'fifties, such as monitoring the enforcement of treaties. But the advance we should seek should be evaluated not in terms of power, but in terms of influence and the expression of opinion. Nobody should underestimate the force of a global forum, even if it chooses to move forward slowly, respecting national differences, and seeking no more than the opportunity to persuade the sovereign states of the world of certain universal priorities.

Is it conceivable that the separate states might see merit in such an arrangement? Can we not set about designing a global framework of democratic opinion-formation which can underpin and reinforce the rights of nations to determine their own development? Can we, indeed, continue to develop our separate national democracies in the difficult environment of world-wide corporations and high technologies, *without* some such general international framework? The peace movement has coined a useful slogan: "think globally, act locally". Will this not be far more susceptible of implementation when there exists a truly global democratic forum?

In spite of the long disputes in the development of such a popular world assembly, these questions seem once again to be relevant at a time of general crisis, which is, perhaps, also a time of new hope.

Footnotes

1. *War: The Offspring of Fear* Reproduced in Stansky: *The Left and the War.* NY OUP 1969 pp. 111-2
2. A. J. P. Taylor: *The Trouble-makers — Dissent over Foreign Policy.* Hamish Hamilton, 1958, pp. 132-5.
3. UN Charter, Chapter XIV, Articles 92-96.
4. cited in J. T. Murphy: *Labour's Big Three.* Bodley Head, 1948, p. 234.
5. Ibid.
6. Ibid, p. 235
7. A. Bullock: *Ernest Bevin — Foreign Secretary 1945-51:* Vol. 3 of the *Life of Ernest Bevin,* Heinemann 1983.
8. See also the same author: *World Peace through World Law.* Harvard, 1958.
9. See A. Martin and J. B. S. Edwards: *The Changing Charter.* Sylvan Press, 1955, pp. 69 et seq.
10. B. Russell: *Common Sense and Nuclear War,* Allen and Unwin, 1959, and B. Russell: *Has Man a Future?* Allen and Unwin, 1961.
11. *Has Man a Future,* p. 81.
12. *Common Sense,* pp. 53 et seq.
13. The Manley-Brandt Report: *Global Challenge,* Pan, 1985, pp.176-7.

Appendix I
Support for Reform

The proposals in this paper were presented at the Cartat Forum in Yugoslavia. Subsequently they were circulated by the UN Secretariat in New York during the meeting of the Third Special Session on Disarmament in June 1988. Various heads of government and leading statesmen have been kind enough to comment on them, and there follows a small selection of their responses.

Prime Minister
New Delhi
June 13, 1988

Dear Mr. Coates,

Thank you for your letter of 21st April enclosing your interesting paper on reform of the United Nations. We share your opinion that we need to think of ways to revitalise and strengthen the international system to make it both more democratic and effective. Your paper is being passed on to our experts to study.

With good wishes,

Yours sincerely,
Rajiv Gandhi

Prime Minister's Office
S-103 33 Stockholm
Sweden

Dear Sir,

Thank you for your letter of 10th February, 1988, together with your paper on reform of the United

Nations structure. I can assure you that your paper will be studied most carefully by the officials in the Ministry for Foreign Affairs dealing with United Nations issues.

The Swedish Government is deeply disturbed by the current problems in the proper functioning of the United Nations, which have manifested themselves above all in serious financial difficulties. It is a matter of high priority for Sweden to participate in constructive efforts to overcome this critical period and to find a new consensus to enable the United Nations system to face the important challenges of the 1990's. Fresh thinking of the kind you offer is most helpful in this respect.

Yours sincerely
Ingvar Carlsson

Minister for Foreign Affairs of Finland

Dear Ken,

Many thanks for your letter of 19 February 1988 and the enclosed draft concerning a reform of the United Nations structure. As you certainly know, Finland is a dedicated supporter of the revitalization and strengthening of the world organization. In this regard, Finland has put forward a number of proposals.

Your ideas seem to deserve careful consideration, since they could on the one hand bring "world opinion" to the attention of the organization and on the other hand strengthen the United Nations vis à vis its Member States. It is evident at the same time that there will be opponents to the proposal for precisely the same reasons.

I am now transferring your proposal for examination by our experts. It so happens that Finland is now a candidate for membership in the Security Council. If elected, we shall have better possibilities than usually to explore the realistic possibilities for strengthening the capabilities of the United Nations.

With best wishes,

Yours sincerely,
Kalevi Sorsa

The Royal Ministry of Foreign Affairs

Dear Mr. Coates,
Your letter of 21 October 1987 to the Prime Minister, Mrs. Brundtland has been forwarded to the Ministry of Foreign Affairs for its consideration.

I found your article of great interest. As you know, Norway is actively involved in the ongoing efforts to strengthen the United Nations and make the organization more effective in its task to ensure world peace and increase international co-operation. The Government of Norway is at present working on a White Paper to Parliament in which Norway's relations with other countries and international organizations are reviewed. Your article provides a stimulating contribution to this work.

Yours Sincerely
Olav Berstad
Acting Head of Division

appendix 1

United Nations

Dear Mr. Coates,

I should like, on behalf of the Secretary-General, to thank you for your letter of 24 March and for sending us a copy of your paper containing your proposal for an elected United Nations consultative assembly.

Peace movements in Europe have indeed played an important role in recent years in raising public awareness and understanding of international peace and security issues, and of the need for concerted action to strengthen the disarmament process.

As you may know, since 1978, the General Assembly has fully recognized the role of world public opinion in promoting specifically the cause of disarmament when it gave leading representatives of non-governmental organizations the opportunity to address it and to submit their views in writing. Their active participation at the forthcoming third special session on disarmament, which will take place here at United Nations Headquarters from 31 May to 25 June 1988, is again encouraged by our Organization. Persistent effort is thus being made by the United Nations to maintain as well as to improve its dialogue with the general public.

I have read with interest your proposal for an elected chamber of the United Nations. As you have already sent your paper to various politicians, I can only suggest that you give it wider circulation. We would certainly be pleased if you will keep us informed of your progress in this effort.

With best wishes.

Yours sincerely,
Yasushi Atashi
Under-Secretary-General
for Disarmament Affairs

Willy Brandt

Dear Sir,

On behalf of Mr. Brandt, who at the moment is not in the country, I have to thank you for your letter and the proposals for a reform of the United Nations.

I think your idea is worth while being considered. Especially I will try to find out a way to bring it to the attention of the West-German delegation to the Special Session of the UN.

Yours sincerely
Klaus-Henning Rosen

Office of Mwalimu Julius K. Nyerere

Dear Mr. Coates

On 31st March this year you kindly sent to Mwalimu Julius K. Nyerere a copy of your proposals about reform of the United Nations. I am ashamed to be replying only now, but still wish to thank you for sending it.

The document was read with interest. There is a probability that the South Commission will, during its life, give some attention to the present structure of the United Nations. Mwalimu — who is, as you doubtless know, the Chairman of the Commission — has therefore decided to send your Paper to the Secretary General so that it can be among the ideas considered at such a time.

With good wishes

Yours Sincerely
Joan E. Wicken
Personal Assistant to Mwalimu Julius K. Nyerere

Appendix II

The Attack on the United Nations

(Excerpts from a Paper by the Rt. Hon. Gough Whitlam, former Prime Minister of Australia)

After a sustained lobby by the Heritage Foundation, first the United States and then Britain withdrew from the United Nations Education, Scientific and Cultural Organisation (UNESCO). Former premier Whitlam analysed the campaign which led up to these defections. His paper shows that the United Nations does not command universal support, and throws much light on the nature of the opposition.

It is timely and proper, in the light of 40 years experience, to review the constitutions of the specialized agencies in respect to the four matters I have discussed — the size of the executive, the tenure of the Directory-General, the revision of the Financial Regulations and the location of conferences. There must be a better way to change the constitution of an organization than by seceding from the organization. It is difficult to discover what the US achieved by withdrawing from ILO through 1978, 1979 and 1980. After the US announced its intention to withdraw from UNESCO, wide ranging reviews of the organization were undertaken by five working groups appointed by the Director-General and by a Temporary Committee established by the Executive Board. There would have been no such reviews if the US had not given notice of withdrawal but the US made no significant contribution to the process of review. Britain, with a new member on the Executive Board and a new Permanent Representative, and France were encouraged by the Western Group to discuss and present proposals. It was as a result of their efforts that the Temporary Committee was set up by the Executive Board in May 1984, at the first of the sessions which it usually holds each year. The Temporary Committee's recommendations were accepted by the Executive Board at its second session, in October, and the Temporary Committee was kept in being to monitor developments for the Executive Board's meetings in 1985. The US refused to join the Temporary Committee and it did not seek to mobilise support for reform among the Third World delegations, to quote a staff report in January 1985 to the Committee on Foreign Affairs of the US House of Representatives. The report declared:

> "By not openly articulating and presenting its reform proposals to Unesco until mid-July, 7 months after the decision to withdraw was announced and 5 months before the date of effective withdrawal, the United States had very little time left to develop and implement an effective plan and strategy to achieve those specific goals. The September meeting of the Executive Board remained the only meeting of a Unesco policy body during 1984 which could begin to consider specific US proposals before the effective date of withdrawal at the end of December 1984. US proposals made in the July 13 letter were made available to the 13-member Temporary Committee at its Third Session in late August, after the TC had already considered a number of similar proposals."

The report is also critical of the performance of the US Ambassador in the handling of the draft GAO report on Unesco, of which selected excerpts were leaked to the media.

The Anglo-French initiatives in the Temporary Committee were remarkably successful. The remarkable thing was not the immensity but the prospect of change. Those who had complained about aspects of Unesco but had done nothing about them now found that it was possible to do something. For the first time for many, many years the Executive Board had been persuaded to accept responsibilities which had always been available to it. The diligence, dedication and dependability of Britain's representatives had merited and achieved widespread support for a change of attitude and direction. The Foreign Office should have been proud of them and appeared to be satisfied. The Americans who had organized the US withdrawal now became desperate. They saw that the US would probably be isolated. They embarked on the same course of action at the end of the second Board session in 1984 as they did at the end of the General Conference in 1983. At the end of the conference the leader and many members of the US delegation expressed their satisfaction with the conduct of the conference, the matters which were discussed and the tone in which they were discussed. They acknowledged the Director-General's helpful attitude. They reported to this effect to Washington. It was then that the campaign started in Washington to persuade the administration to give notice to withdrawal. At the end of the second Board session in 1984 the same Americans decided to bypass the Foreign Office and to use the British media to persuade the British Government to give notice to withdrawal.

The Commonwealth permanent delegates stationed in Paris were the first to spot what was going on in Britain. They listen to the BBC. They read the English newspapers. They have English textbooks and reference books on their shelves. They usually had part of their higher education in Britain. They noticed that after the second Board session the same arguments and attitudes about Unesco were appearing in the British Media as had appeared in the US media at the end of the previous year. The similarity in the campaigns was no coincidence. The International Organizations section of the State Department had engaged the same organization to conduct both campaigns, the Heritage Foundation, which is described in its letter-head as "a tax-exempt, public policy research institute". It is very rich and, to my mind, a very sinister organization. It was established in 1973. It claims to have organized the agenda of the first and later the second Reagan Administrations. Robert Chessyre wrote from Washington in the *Observer* of 25 November 1984:

> "Heritage backers include Reagan's friend, brewer Joseph Coors, and the most shadowy of American right-wing philanthropists, Richard Mellon Scaife, a scion of the Mellon banking family."

Time elaborated on 3 December 1984:

> "Heritage was founded with a grant of $250,000 from Joseph Coors, the Colorado brewing magnate and backer of conservative causes. Today it receives about a third of its $10 million annual budget from foundations, many of them begun by ideological sympathizers like Pittsburgh money-man Richard Mellon Scaife and Industrialist John Olin. Another third is contributed by business corporations, ... The final third comes from 130,000 individual donors."

All contributions are tax-deductable.

The Heritage Foundation's hostility towards the UN system can be seen from the titles of some of its recent publications:

The International Labor Organization: Mirroring The UN's Problems (1982)

UNCTAD: An Organisation Betraying Its Mission (1983)

The Food and Agriculture Organization: A Flawed Strategy In the War Against Hunger (1984)

A World Without a UN: What Would Happen If the United Nations Shut Down (1984)

The World Health Organization: Resisting Third

appendix 2

World Ideological Pressures (1985)
The United Nations Development Program: Failing the World's Poor (1985)

To spearhead its campaign against Unesco, the Foundation employed Associate Professor Owen Harries, who in September 1981 had become an Australian citizen and the Australian Ambassador to Unesco. After taking up his duties in Paris he saw much of the new American Ambassador to Unesco, Jean Gerard, and made three visits to the US, each time visiting the Heritage Foundation in Washington DC. In September 1983 he became John M. Olin Fellow at the Foundation. The president of the Foundation, Edwin J. Feulner Jr., claims that "the President's decision to withdraw from Unesco was a direct result of a paper by Owen Harries that detailed a long list of shocking abuses". For several weeks after Christmas 1983 Harries was engaged in justifying America's withdrawal. In October 1984 he was engaged in promoting Britain's withdrawal. In three London gatherings of which I am aware he was supported by Mrs Gerard.

The concluding meetings of the Unesco Executive Board were held on 18, 19, 20 and 22 October. Although Mrs Gerard was one of its Vice-Presidents and had pending resolutions on the agenda, she was away in London on 18, 19 and 20 October and flew back to London immediately after the meeting on 22 October. A dinner at the Garrick Club on Friday, 19 October was attended by:

Mrs Jean Gerard; Mr Owen Harries; Lord Bauer; Lord Beloff; Lord Chalfont; Mr Michael Charlton, BBC; Mr Richard Hoggart; Mr Roger Scruton, weekly columnist, *The Times;* Mr Huw Wheldon, ex-BBC.

Apologies were received from Mr Paul Johnson.

A dinner at the Brooks Club on 22 October was attended by:

Mrs Jean Gerard; Mr Owen Harries; Lord Bauer; Mr Brian Beedham, foreign editor, *Economist*; Mr Charles Douglas-Hume, editor, *The Times*; Mr Dirk Kinane, US citizen in Unesco Secretariat; Mr Gerald Mansell, ex-BBC; Mr Roger Scruton.

On Tuesday evening 23 October, Mrs Gerard and Mr Harries took part in a discussion at the Royal Overseas League arranged by the Institute of European Defence and Strategic Studies. Over 40 persons accepted invitations to attend, including from the media (e.g. Rosemary Righter) and the House of Commons (e.g. Sir Peter Blaker). There may well have been other gatherings, but I have cited only the three of which I have been told by persons who were present. Not all those who were present sympathized with the anti-Unesco sentiments advanced by Mrs Gerard and Mr Harries. Mr Harries also had lunch with Mr Douglas-Hume.

The cultivation of the media was most effective. Previously there had been very few editorials and signed articles on Unesco. Between the Gerard/Harries foray and Sir Geoffry Howe's announcement of withdrawal on 22 November, there was a spate of them. I have learned of the following:

21 October	*Sunday Times*
22 October	*Daily Telegraph*
24 October	*Daily Mail*
	The Times
27 October	*Spectator*
29 October	*Daily Telegraph*
30 October	*Financial Times*
3 November	*The Times*
5 November	*The Times*
7 November	*Daily Telegraph*
10 November	*Spectator*
11 November	*Observer*

15 November	*Guardian*
16 November	*The Times*
	Guardian
	Yorkshire Post
17 November	*Economist*
18 November	*Sunday Times*
	Mail on Sunday
19 November	*Daily Telegraph*
	Daily Mirror
20 November	*Guardian*
	The Times
21 November	*Guardian*
	The Times
	Daily Telegraph
22 November	*Daily Mail*
	Guardian

Of outstanding distinction was the article by Lord Chalfont, who gave an initial taste for foreign affairs to readers of the editorial page of the *Mail on Sunday* with an article entitled "Mad Hatters Nonsense Factory". One must dismiss the thought that the noble lord had plagiarized an article by Harries on the "Mad Hatter's tea party" in the October *Readers Digest;* it would be ludicrous to suggest that he gets his own ideas and words from the *Digest* — or from the *Mail.*

On 15 November, 38 Commonwealth High Commissioners met in London and decided that their Dean should send a letter to Sir Geoffrey Howe to support Britain's continuing membership of Unesco. This is the first time that High Commissioners have made such a demarche to a Foreign Secretary. Sir Geoffry met them on 21 November. They were too late. He announced Britain's withdrawal in the Commons the next day.

Midway through the press campaign questions on Unesco were placed on the Order Paper of the House of Commons. Western delegates in Unesco were disturbed by messages from their colleagues in London about these questions. At several of the Western group meetings they expressed and reiterated a unanimous view that a notice of withdrawal by Britain would probably stop the process of reform in its tracks. They said that there would be a backlash against Western countries and that the developing countries would believe that they had been deceived. Having heard these views without demur, Mrs Gerard proceeded to make her visits to London to promote the very course of action which her colleagues feared and deplored. Not only did she not tell her British colleagues that she was going to London, but she did not tell them what she had done after she returned. Lack of candour led to lack of trust and lack of progress in the Western group.

After 22 November the flurry of interest in Unesco in the media and in the Commons subsided as completely and rapidly as it had erupted. I have given details of events and persons in order to explain how a major change was brought about in British policy towards the UN system over the space of five weeks through American hustlers using the British press and backbenchers to stampede the British Government. Few would have thought that a British Government was so vulnerable and the British press so manipulable.

Let me first examine the implications within Unesco. There can be no doubt that a government can make decisions on foreign policy as on any other matters without or despite the views of its official advisers. There can be no doubt that an ambassador can pursue his or her government's objectives as he or she sees fit or his or her government allows.

Nevertheless a government depends on its ambassadors and other diplomatic representatives to pursue its objectives in other capitals and particularly in multilateral organizations. In February 1985 the Chairman of the Executive Board called a special session. The British Representatives were unchanged. They were still as dedicated, diligent and dependable as before but their influence had been eliminated. No other Board member was prepared to take a lead from them. Why should the representatives of other countries support them when their own government did not? In American parlance, they were lame ducks. It was now left to other members of the Board to sustain the initiatives that Britain and France had initiated.

Britain's precipitate action was soon seen to have implications for the whole UN system. Britain was an original member of the UN and of all its specialized agencies. Distinguished Britons, Sir John Boyd Orr and Sir Julian Huxley, had been the foundation Directors-General of FAO and Unesco and another, Wilfred Jenks, had been Director-General of the ILO in the early 1970s. Britain is a permanent member of the Security Council and the custodian of the Unesco Constitution. The world may be accustomed to the US striking out from time to time at the World Court, the specialized agencies and the international banks. It is novel and uncharacteristic for the UK to do so. The UK now joined with the US in breaching the universal membership of the UN system. At the same time as it notified its withdrawal from Unesco it succumbed, with the Federal Republic of Germany (FRG), to American pressure in refusing to sign the Law of the Sea Convention, another target of the Heritage Foundation.

The campaign to preserve British membership of Unesco is a first and essential step in preserving the universality of the UN system. There are certain criticisms of Unesco which must be countered forthwith. The organisation has had a bad press because it has been a forum for criticisms of the wire services. Your newspapers, including the Australian-owned ones, constantly suggest that the New World Information and Communication Order (NWICO), which the UN General Assembly entrusted to Unesco, would lead to censorship of the press, licensing of journalists and the establishment of government papers in competition with private ones. The simple fact is that if Unesco aimed to do any of these things it would first have to adopt a convention and then Member States would have to ratify that convention. The convention would only operate in those countries that ratified it. No steps have been taken to draft such a convention. Unesco has passed no resolutions and made no appropriations for any of the purposes alleged. The reaction of the 1980 General Conference to the McBride Report was, at the timely instigation of the Director-General, to establish the International Program for the Development of Communication (IPDC).

A justification given for Britain's notice of withdrawal was to save money or to spend it better. As a matter of fact the UK makes a profit out of Unesco, principally because the Americans have made English the number one language in the world. Accordingly, if experts are needed in a great number of fields, particularly to write or edit or assemble publications or programmes in the English language, Unesco seeks experts from across the Channel. In financial terms Britain gets very much more out of Unesco than it puts in. Yet the UK has joined with the US in taking the biggest step in their history to diminish the influence of the English-speaking world in relation to the French- and Spanish-speaking worlds, which staunchly support Unesco.

Acknowledgements

Part of Chapter 1 was published in *The Most Dangerous Decade*, Spokesman, 1984. Chapters 4 and 6 were first published in *ENDpapers*, Numbers 13 and 14. Chapter 2 was prepared for the Third International Conference of Nuclear-Free Local Authorities in Perugia, in 1986. Chapter 4 was prepared for the Conference of Anti-nuclear Networks in Tokyo, in 1986. Chapter 5 was a paper presented in Paris at an international University Conference in 1986. Chapter 7 was a paper presented at the Conference on Socialism in the World, Cavtat, Yugoslavia, 1987.

Versions of these papers have variously appeared in publications in Australia, France, Denmark, Italy, India, Yugoslavia and Japan.